"Del Duduit has collected wonderful gems of faith from a variety of MLB's best players and coaches who are dedicated to bringing glory to Christ and shining their light for Him. They provide true examples of Christian mentorship to baseball fans of all generations. *Dugout Devotions* is a grand slam!"

—Blaine Boyer, MLB pitcher

"*Dugout Devotions* features wonderful testimonies from some of the biggest names in the MLB. The stories bring out the best sides of the players and coaches and, most of all, lift up the name of the Lord. I'm humbled to be a part of it."

—Clint Hurdle, manager of the Pittsburgh Pirates

"Faith and baseball have always been important in my life. As a kid, I wanted to play professional baseball, but God had a different plan for my life. I always loved hearing stories of how faith played a major role in the lives of some of our most famous major leaguers—those stories encouraged me. My friend and author, Del Duduit, takes examples from some of baseball's greatest players and compiles their stories of faith into an encouraging devotional that I highly recommend."

—Congressman Bill Johnson, Ohio

"Encouraging, inspirational, and impactful . . . Del Duduit has delivered another home run. Packed full of poignant personal testimonies from some of the game's biggest stars, *Dugout Devotions* provides valuable spiritual fodder for a deeper walk with God."

—John Huang, Nolan Media Group

"Del Duduit has a knack for translating sports action into vibrant devotionals. He's done it again with *Dugout Devotions*. Jumping off from interviews with the biggest names in baseball, Del shows us how to put God first."

—David L. Winters, author of *Taking God to Work*

"Keep in mind that I was a professional boxer and faced some tough opponents in the ring. But this devotional hit a home run for me, and I gained valuable spiritual insight inside this inspirational book about baseball and the Lord. For me, *Dugout Devotions* is a total knock out."

—Mark Frazie, former professional boxer, known as the "Golden Boy"

"Like a veteran coach, Del engages the heart first and then boldly challenges us to action. Each devotional used the Word of God and the platform of sport to capture my attention and concluded with an array of practical steps on how to apply what I just learned. Outstanding!"

—Brian Smith, Athletes in Action, author of
The Assist: A Gospel-Centered Guide to Glorifying God through Sports

"Baseball. Great players. Unforgettable conversations. Life lessons. God, faith, and family. All of this and more are here in *Dugout Devotions*. Del Duduit knows how to get the story and pull out the best from it. His one-on-one interviews with some of today's best players and the life applications he makes from those will inspire and enrich your walk with God and your relationships with others. Step into the dugout, learn the lessons these devotions provide, and then get back onto the field of life. The quality of your play is sure to improve."

—William D. Watkins, award-winning writer, editor, teacher, and speaker

"Del intentionally moves beyond just being a solid storyteller into deeper waters. He encourages us to think more and live differently! Each chapter offers something to chew on beyond the inspirational details of the players' lives, mining each narrative for truths applicable to everyone's life. Should be plenty to think about after reading this book!"

—Ed Uszynski, lead strategist/content developer, Athletes in Action

"Del knocked it out of the park with *Dugout Devotions*. The stories are inspiring, and the spiritual application is impactful. Even if you're not a diehard enthusiast of America's favorite pastime, you'll be touched because these are stories that linger in your heart."

—Bethany Jett, author of *The Cinderella Rule*

DUGOUT
DEVOTIONS

INSPIRATIONAL HITS FROM MLB'S BEST

DEL DUDUIT

IRON STREAM
B O O K S
An imprint of Iron Stream Media
Birmingham, Alabama

Iron Stream Books
5184 Caldwell Mill Rd.
St. 204-221
Hoover, AL 35244
NewHopePublishers.com
IronStreamMedia.com
New Hope® Publishers and Iron Stream Books are imprints of Iron Stream Media

Iron Stream Media serves its authors as they express their views, which may not express
the views of the publisher.

Library of Congress Cataloging-in-Publication Data

Names: Duduit, Del, 1966- editor.
Title: Dugout devotions : inspirational hits from MLB's best / [edited by]
Del Duduit.
Description: First [edition]. | Birmingham : New Hope Publishers, 2018.
Identifiers: LCCN 2018043987 | ISBN 9781563091339 (permabind)
Subjects: LCSH: Christian life. | Spiritual life--Christianity. | Baseball
players--Religious life. | Baseball--Religious aspects--Christianity.
Classification: LCC BV4501.3 .D838 2018 | DDC 242/.68--dc23
LC record available at https://lccn.loc.gov/2018043987

Copyright information continues on page 147.

Cover photo: Dennis E. Atchenson II

ISBN-13: 978-1-56309-133-9

1 2 3 4 5—23 22 21 20 19

This book is dedicated to my oldest son Gabe.

You have turned out to be a wonderful example of a fine Christian man with a beautiful family. Everyone who knows you tells me how much they enjoy your preaching and your sense of humor. I agree, but am also partial to your ability and talent to cook.

Over the past year, while I have written this book, I reflected back on our time together as father and son, when you played baseball and I was one of your coaches.

I may have been tough on you at times, as most fathers are on their own, but I hope you had fun and entertain fond memories.

I recall your graceful belly-flop slides into second base and have vivid memories of your first home run in a game in Stockdale, Ohio.

One of my most cherished memories was when we took a day trip to Chicago to watch the Cubs play at historic Wrigley Field. Sammy Sosa blasted three dingers that day, and later we ate deep-dish pizza at Pizzeria Uno on Ohio Street.

But perhaps the most significant memory I have of you is not related to sports. I was alone on business in a hotel room in Parkersburg, West Virginia, in 2017. I was in bed, and my phone buzzed. You sent a text message on March 21 at 11:08 p.m. and told me how proud you were of me for pursuing my passion to write this book.

I'll always keep that text, and it inspires me when I get down. This is one reason I dedicate the first book in this series to you, Gabe.

Your love for baseball does not compare to your desire to be a wonderful Christian son, husband, and father—that means everything to your mom and me.

I love you and am beyond proud to be your dad. You'll never know how you inspire me to be better, every day.

Dad

The following people played a vital role in the completion of this book. I would like to personally thank them.

My wife Angie, for being my first editor and supporting me through the proposal process.

My agent Cyle Young for his assistance in getting this book in front of the right people and for contributing devotionals for this book.

Chris Slone, the former editor of the *Portsmouth Daily Times* in Portsmouth, Ohio, for assisting with media credentials.

Blaine Boyer, for writing the foreword and for being a friend.

Clint Hurdle, for his promotional support and prayers.

Michelle Medlock Adams for contributing devotionals.

Ryan Farr for contributing devotionals.

Beckie Lindsey for contributing devotionals.

Scott McCausey for contributing devotionals.

Clint Rutledge for contributing devotionals.

Bill Watkins for the inspiration to write this book.

Mark Householder, Ed Uszynski, Brian Smith, and Athletes in Action for providing support and opportunities.

Ramona Richards and John Herring with Iron Stream Books for allowing me to present this idea to you at the Florida Christian Writers Conference.

God, for making this all possible.

CONTENTS

FOREWORD

Professional baseball players get a lot of attention from their fans for the feats they accomplish on the field. If you hear the names Babe Ruth, Hank Aaron, or Reggie Jackson, you immediately think about home runs. The names Nolan Ryan, Randy Johnson, and Jake Arrieta remind us of great pitching. Other names, such as Derek Jeter, might bring to mind great championship games of the World Series.

But what about their personal lives? What about their relationships with Jesus Christ? After you read *Dugout Devotions*, some of the great baseball names will leave a different impression on you. For instance, when you hear the name Andy Pettitte, you think of the mighty Yankee dynasty and its world championship rings. In this book, you find out about a time when telling the truth was the right thing for Andy to do, even though it put his career in jeopardy.

Then there's Brian Dozier. You probably know him as an All-Star second baseman for the Los Angeles Dodgers. After reading this devotional, you'll find out how he grew stronger as a Christian when life got tough during his college years.

You will also get to know Clint Hurdle as more than a manager for the Pittsburgh Pirates. He is a man dedicated to encouraging not only his ball team but also a large private network of close friends with daily inspirational messages.

Aaron Judge is a larger-than-life All-Star outfielder for the New York Yankees, but did you know he treasures his faith more than his pinstripes?

Dugout Devotions also features multiple Cy Young Award-winner Clayton Kershaw, multiple MLB MVP Albert Pujols, and World Series MVP Ben Zobrist, among other All-Stars. These are just a few examples of the baseball icons you will get to know better through reading this book. You will also hear about my good friend Adam Wainwright and find out about my own personal testimony.

Del Duduit has collected some wonderful gems of faith from a variety of MLB's best players and coaches who are dedicated to bringing glory to Christ and shining their light for Him. They provide a true example of Christian mentorship to baseball fans of all generations.

Blaine Boyer
MLB Pitcher

DAY 1
GROW THROUGH YOUR CHALLENGES

Brian Dozier
All-Star Second Baseman
Los Angeles Dodgers

By Del Duduit

You have delivered me from all my troubles, and my eyes
have looked in triumph on my foes.

—Psalm 54:7

"I didn't know it at the time, but what I went through was
a true blessing in disguise," Brian Dozier said. "The Lord
knew what He was doing, but I didn't at the time."

It appeared to be the right decision. Brian passed on
the MLB draft, opting instead to stay at the University of
Southern Mississippi to finish his senior year and earn his
degree. He was a sure-fire bet to make it in the big leagues.
He made All-American his freshman year. In 224 career
college games, he posted a .355 average with fifty-five dou-
bles and seven triples, along with sixteen home runs. In
2009, he led his squad to the College World Series.

During his senior year, he dove to make a play and shattered his collarbone.

Eight screws and a plate were inserted into his right shoulder, putting his dreams of playing in the major leagues in serious doubt.

Maybe he made the wrong decision after all. Maybe he should have gone to Major League Baseball when he first had the chance.

"I tell you what, I went through some real struggles," he said. "I had turned down the draft and just assumed it would be there the next year. I never thought I'd bust up my shoulder."

Have you ever been in a similar situation and taken your future for granted? What would you do? Would you give up or keep going?

It's no coincidence Brian's favorite character in the Bible is Job. He doesn't compare himself to Job, but he admires his perseverance and determination to live for the Lord no matter what happened to him.

"I learned through all of that and by what Job went through to rely on God through everything—especially the bad times," he said. "There are times when we get angry and question, but you have to count on Him to get you through."

Brian did what only he could do. He waited and learned.

He learned how to be a true leader without being on the field. He encouraged those who could perform and gave advice to younger players.

He slowly developed an attitude similar to William Wallace in his favorite movie *Braveheart*.

"Never let them see you sweat," he said. "Even when you are down, always be positive and strong."

He carried this attitude with him while going through physical therapy. Finally, the MLB draft drew near.

"I didn't know what to think because I was hurt," he said. "I didn't know if anyone would take me."

The Minnesota Twins selected him in the eighth round of the draft in 2009. He wasn't a disappointment. In fact, he exceeded all expectations.

In 2014, he became the first second baseman in the history of the team to record a 20/20 season (more than twenty home runs and more than twenty stolen bases). He scored the second-most runs in a season (112) since the record-high in 1997. The next year, fans selected him as a replacement in the MLB All-Star game. He had an immediate impact when he smacked a home run in his first at bat in the eighth inning.

In 2016, Brian became the first American League second baseman to hit forty home runs in a season.

"I'm so grateful the Twins gave me this opportunity," he said. "And I'm grateful I serve a God who never gives up on us."

His waiting and learning paid off. Perhaps he became more aware and appreciative during his time off the field. He loves the fact that Jesus taught him a valuable lesson during his recovery.

"That time I was hurt was a wonderful growing experience for me," he said. "I don't know if I'd be the leader I am today had it not been for that."

What lessons did you learn during your trials? Did you grow during your troubles or hide from them?

Not only so, but we also glory in our sufferings, because we
know that suffering produces perseverance.

—Romans 5:3

On Deck

Prepare yourself to deal with tough times by studying and
reading the Word of God. Once there, you will find the
will of the Master and learn to face life's difficulties. The
Book of Job will teach patience and trust. I hope you do
not go through what Job did. But if you even come close,
take note of how he handled horrible situations. It would
have been easy to "curse God and die," but he chose to
follow, wait, and trust. In the end, Job received his reward
many times over, "The Spirit of God has made me; the
breath of the Almighty gives me life" (Job 33:4).

Step Up to the Plate

If by chance you find yourself in a similar circumstance
like Brian's, how will you cope with it? His dreams were
on the verge of being shattered, and his goal of playing in
the MLB was in serious jeopardy. But he took a positive
approach and became a true leader. He never let his team
see him sweat, even though inside he may have been a ner-
vous wreck.

When circumstances seem impossible, trust God more
than ever and lead the way. Try these seven simple actions.

1. Get out of the way. Put aside your ways and expectations and surrender to His plans.
2. Cry out to the Lord. If you reach out in humility and sincerity, He will hear you.
3. Flee from evil. Separate yourself from negative influences. Avoid those who may drag you down.
4. Make God first in your life. It's easy to put yourself and your needs at the top of the list. A good way to start is by tithing. Give God the first 10 percent of your paycheck. Trust Him the way Job did.
5. Get into the Word of God. There you will witness the Lord's heart and yours too. You might not like what you find out about yourself, but it will help you become a better person.
6. Listen to the Spirit. As you go through your day, try to hear what God tells you. Questions and doubts may arise, but the Holy Spirit won't ever take you down the wrong path. "Whoever heeds discipline shows the way to life, but whoever ignores correction leads others astray" (Proverbs 10:17).
7. Find comfort in His Love. This step is the best. Here you find how much He really does love and care for you. Put your complete trust in the Lord and listen to His calling.

These steps are not always easy to follow, but try them. Develop Brian's "never let them see you sweat" attitude, and trust in the Lord. You might be injured, and there may be disappointments. But when it's all said and done, God can prepare you to get back on the field.

DAY 2

WHAT IS THE MOST IMPORTANT THING IN LIFE?

Albert Pujols
Multiple MVP Winner and First Baseman
Los Angeles Angels of Anaheim

By Del Duduit

> For I am not ashamed of the gospel of Christ: for it is the
> power of God unto salvation to every one that believeth;
> to the Jew first, and also to the Greek.
>
> —Romans 1:16 KJV

"I just want to encourage the guys I meet in this game and let them know they can stay strong in their faith," Albert Pujols said. "Never lose your relationship with God."

When runners make it to first base against the Angels, they hear a question from the three-time National League MVP.

"What is the most important thing in life?" he asks.

Some reply that God is a priority while others mention family, and some don't even know what to say. How would you respond if a two-time World Series champion posed this question to you?

For Albert, he feels his job as a Christian is to challenge everyone he meets, especially at first base where he spends a great deal of his time. He spent the first ten years of his professional career with the St. Louis Cardinals and joined the Los Angeles Angels in 2012.

"I represent a great organization with the Angels," he said. "But I believe I serve my Lord above all, and I need to share my testimony with others."

When he first came into the MLB, he was not a believer. "I didn't know anything about Him other than He might exist," he said. "But I never had that relationship with Him until I was presented the gospel."

His wife Deidra and his grandmother introduced him to Christ. Now he feels it is his privilege and calling to tell others about the goodness of God.

"My life's goal is to bring glory to Jesus," he said. "My life is not somewhat dedicated to the Lord, it's a 100-percent commitment to Jesus and to His will."

God has blessed Albert with tremendous athletic ability, and Albert gives Him all the credit for the talents that allow him to serve as an ambassador on the diamond.

"I use this as my platform to elevate the name of Jesus Christ," he said. "Some have TV and some have radio and a pulpit—I use the baseball field."

He also knows the difference between saying you're a Christian and living a true example of righteousness.

"This is not a religious thing to me," he said. "This is about letting God take control of your life and use you to bring glory to His name."

And Albert capitalizes on every opportunity he can to praise God. If people don't get a chance to hear him talk about the Lord, his spikes still present the message of Christ—Philippians 4:13 appears on one shoe, and the other displays Romans 5:19.

His priority is to make sure everyone he comes into contact with knows he serves a loving God.

For as by one man's disobedience many were made sinners, so by the obedience of one shall many be made righteous.
—Romans 5:19 KJV

Albert was named the *Sports Illustrated* Player of the Decade as well as the *Sporting News* Player of the Decade in 2009, and his induction into the Baseball Hall of Fame is inevitable. In addition, he has earned two World Series rings, but he wants more than ever to make sure he gets a robe and crown when his life on earth is over. His priorities are in line.

On Deck

Imagine you are playing against the Angels, and it's your turn at bat. You're facing Ricky Nolasco, and the count is 2-2. Here comes the fast ball, and you take it up the middle for a base hit. You round first base and clap your hands to celebrate. You slap the first base coach's hand and gather yourself to get your lead. Then you hear Albert. "What is the most important thing in your life?"

What will your answer be? The time for celebration is over. He deserves an answer. God deserves an answer.

Now, let's get back to reality. You take your ten-year-old son fishing. You find a nice shady spot and settle in for a relaxing day. You open up the picnic basket and pull out bologna sandwiches and chips to share. You bait the hook and fling the line into the pond. It's just the two of you.

Then you see the bobber go up and down, and you get all excited. "Hook him, hook him," you instruct your son. "Give him some line, and now reel," you continue.

Finally, your boy brings in the blue gill. You hold up the fish, celebrate, and take pictures. It's the first catch of the day. You slowly put it back in the water. You are so happy. Then your son asks you out of nowhere, "Dad, what's the most important thing in life?"

What will your answer be? The time for celebration is over. He deserves an answer. God deserves an answer.

Step Up to the Plate

The best response in both scenarios is to say you want a personal relationship with Christ, and you want everyone in your family to have one too. If you need to be a better witness for the Lord, follow these five steps:

1. Make sure you are filled with the Spirit of God and are in a right relationship with Him before you share your testimony with others. Maintain a close relationship with Jesus Christ so you can share the good news.
2. Seek and pray for opportunities. Don't force your beliefs on others. Simply pray for an opening to present itself, and it will. God may choose a time that catches you off guard, so always be prepared. "Be wise in the way you act toward outsiders; make the most of every opportunity" (Colossians 4:5).

3. Be genuine. Like the old saying often attributed to Teddy Roosevelt says, "Nobody cares how much you know, until they know how much you care." If you put on a show, people will know. Be real, humble, authentic, and honest.
4. Pose a question—just like Albert does. Ask them what they lack. Ask if they have peace. Ask if they are ready to begin a new life.
5. Call to action. You have shared the gospel and lived the example. You have earned the right to invite the person to Christ. If they say no, don't push; simply encourage. Speak in love, and show them there is a better life. God died for our sins so we may have eternal life.

These are only suggestions. Not every situation will be the same. But it is our job to show everyone the love of God. You may not earn a World Series ring in your lifetime, but you can receive a jewel in your crown when you get to heaven by sharing the good news of Christ.

DAY 3
FIND YOUR IDENTITY IN CHRIST

Ben Zobrist
MVP Second Baseman
Chicago Cubs

By Michelle Medlock Adams

I have been crucified with Christ. It is no longer I who
live, but Christ who lives in me. And the life I now live in
the flesh I live by faith in the Son of God, who loved me
and gave himself for me.

—Galatians 2:20 ESV

Sports celebrities are everywhere—on giant billboards, in television commercials and movies, and hanging out with A-list
celebrities.

Fans wear the jerseys of their favorite players and dedicate
entire websites in their honor. Sportscasters compare them to
former greats in their designated sport. Once these stellar athletes really "make it," they might even get their picture on the
front of a cereal box or have their own collectible action figure
created in their honor.

But Ben Zobrist, standout second baseman for the Chicago
Cubs, knows fame is fleeting. You can be the MVP of a World
Series Championship team one day—which he was in 2016—
and booed by fans the next game if you're having an off day at

bat. Bottom line, you can't be moved by the cheers or the jeers. Neither of those defines you, according to Ben.

You can't believe everything the sportswriters write about you, but you can believe what the Word of God says about you.

Your identity must be in Christ alone.

Ben has experienced both the highs and lows that often accompany a high-profile athlete. In the 2016 World Series, he drove in the Cubs go-ahead run on a double down the left-field line in the tenth inning, ending the team's 108-year drought. He went on to become the MVP of the World Series after dominating with ten hits, batting .357 in all seven games. It was magical. It was a moment in sports history people will talk about forever. Fast forward to 2017, and it's a very different scenario. Ben was plagued with wrist and back injuries and posted a career-worst .232 batting average. Obviously, that had to be frustrating for such a talented ballplayer, but he cheered from the dugout as he nursed his injuries. So how did he keep such a great attitude during one of the most difficult seasons of his life? By realizing his worth isn't based on his batting average.

"Your life is not about what you can become—it's about who God says you are—based on what Christ has done," he says. "And through Christ you can be holy, pure, perfect, lovely, everything you want to be—not by your own effort but because Christ already accomplished that—it was all on your behalf—so you can be a child of God and a child of the King of kings and Lord of lords. That's an incredible feeling."

Ben, like other professional athletes, says he has struggled with his identity at times throughout his career. He admits it's sometimes tough to keep it all in perspective.

"Fighting the idolatry of putting my identity in what I do on a baseball field—taking joy in that—instead of taking joy in the fact that I'm a child of God," he explains, is difficult. Ultimately, though, he says, "Winning games and awards is nice, but gaining my ultimate reward in heaven is what I really work for."

Ben wants to be recognized as much for his Christian witness as he is for his amazing feats on the field. For him, that would be true success.

"I don't have anything to boast about—there is nothing I can say I've done. I can say my biggest success is Christ did things through me. That's my success. He has a hold of me and I put my hands in His—I need Him every day. If people can identify Christ in me then I am being a successful Christian."

There's an old church camp song that says, "They'll know we are Christians by our love," and Ben hopes his life—on and off the field—is a reflection of those simple, yet powerful lyrics. Of course, that little chorus is based on John 13:35 that says, "By this everyone will know that you are my disciples, if you love one another."

Living the love. Not being moved by good or bad press. Appreciating the fan support, awards, and victories, but not letting them define you. Those are the directives that keep Ben grounded, focused, humble, and truly content with his life.

"You are created by God and for God—and you will not be at peace and you won't find true joy in your life until you allow Him to be a part of it," he says. "God is the only way to have true happiness."

On Deck

If you struggle with your own identity, often wondering who you are, allowing others to define you, then get into the Word and find out who God says you are! He says you're the head and not the tail (Deuteronomy 28:13). He says you're a victor, not a victim (1 Corinthians 15:57). He says you're an overcomer (1 John 5:4–5). He says you're a child of the Most-High God and heir of God (Galatians 4:7)! Like Ben, train your mind to focus on who you are in Christ Jesus, tuning out all the other voices—good and bad. Don't let your job performance, your accolades, your victories, or your defeats determine who you are. Instead, search the Bible and meditate on these Scripture passages and many others that define you according to your Heavenly Father such as Jeremiah 1:5a; John 1:12; 1 Corinthians 6:17; 1 Corinthians 12:27; Ephesians 1:5; and 1 Peter 2:9, to name a few.

Step Up to the Plate

If you battle with feelings of inferiority or feelings of superiority, lay them at the Father's feet today. Ask Him to help you see yourself through His eyes. Don't be moved by negative or positive words spoken about you. Instead, get your eyes off yourself and onto your Heavenly Father. Let God affirm you. Let God love on you. Let God define you. Second Corinthians 1:22 (NLT) says, "He has identified us as his own by placing the Holy Spirit in our hearts." In other words, you are identified by God and God alone. Think about this truth and possibly journal your answer to this question: Would your life be different if you truly accepted the fact that God approves of you and has called you His precious child?

DAY 4
FINDING VALUE IN LIFE'S DAILY GRIND

Clayton Kershaw
Multiple Cy Young Award-Winning Pitcher
Los Angeles Dodgers

By Clint Rutledge

> Whatever you do, work at it with all your heart, as working for the Lord, not for human masters.
> —Colossians 3:23

One night, when Clayton Kershaw and his wife Ellen returned home from a social event around 10 p. m., she innocently suggested he wait and do his workout the next day. He replied that his teammates would have put in the work today and he did not want to get a day behind. This is the kind of work ethic that has made him one of the best pitchers in all of Major League Baseball.

He worked his way through the Dodgers' farm system and reached the majors at the ripe age of twenty years old. He debuted his career in 2008 as the youngest player in Major League Baseball. In 2011, he won the pitching Triple Crown and the National League Cy Young Award, becoming the youngest pitcher to accomplish either of these feats since Dwight Gooden in 1985. On June 18, 2014, he accomplished another career milestone by pitching his first major league no-hitter. Not one of these accomplishments happened because he just showed up to pitch one day.

Of course, he is blessed with God-given ability. The average person cannot throw a fastball over ninety miles per hour and then drop in a curve or a devastating slider for good measure. However, there are many people who have been blessed with talent in one form or another, but they have failed to cultivate it with hard work and discipline. Clayton, on the other hand, has accepted his gift and worked to do something with it. He refuses to take a break, so it's no wonder his favorite Scripture verse is Colossians 3:23, "Whatever you do, work at it with all your heart, as working for the Lord, not for human masters."

"If you are working for the Lord, great things will happen," he says. "I work hard every day at this game, and I also want to work hard for the Lord. This helps me to remember what God did for me and puts things into proper perspective. Life is a grind just like baseball. You have to work hard at it and then get up the next day and work hard at it again."

Veteran catcher Brad Ausmus notes that Clayton is religious about sticking to his routine in the bullpen whether he feels great or not. He has only seen one other player prepare the same way—Roger Clemens, the "Rocket," and seven-time Cy Young award winner. While some pitchers throw in the bullpen until everything feels right, Clayton takes a different approach. When asked about his strategy once during an interview, he simply smiled and said, "You gotta save your bullets—you're not getting anybody out in the bullpen." His perspective is he wants to work hard, follow his routine, and be ready to do his best for his team when it comes time for him to start.

His approach to baseball brings up a good question for all of us. How often do we spend time working hard at things that don't matter? We are a nation of busy people and run from one place to the next, one practice to the next, one game to the next, one event to the next. We often fail to slow down long enough to even eat dinner with our families. We find ourselves maxed out, stressed out, and worn out. Maybe it's time to "save our bullets" as Clayton would say. Save them for the times when it really matters.

He believes there is a higher calling for all of us, if we will listen. When asked how he wanted people to remember him, Clayton replied, "The applause and awards are great, but those are all earthly things. Don't get me wrong; I love them, and I appreciate them. I am like anyone else. I love getting rewarded for hard work, but ultimately the impact you can have on people is the most important thing."

He says he and his wife try to focus on showing his two children the right way to live. Perhaps we should be saving our bullets for this purpose. We all hang up our cleats one day. For some, that day comes earlier than others, but it will eventually come for everyone. When your kids hang up their cleats, what will their perspective be on life? Will sports be the only thing they know? Will they struggle because their self-worth has always been determined by how they play rather than who they are?

> And let us not grow weary of doing good, for in due season we will reap, if we do not give up. So then, as we have opportunity, let us do good to everyone, and especially to those who are of the household of faith.
>
> —Galatians 6:9–10 ESV

How about you? What are you doing that makes God smile? What are you doing that you have been called to do? What positive impact are you having on the lives of others? You should be saving your bullets to work for the Lord. No matter if you are pitching, parenting, or playing the game of life, you must do it all with an intentionality that says, "Today I am going to work hard. And I am going to do it as though I am working for the Lord."

On Deck

Identify areas of opportunity; list them out. Jotting them down on paper is a great way to remind yourself of your goals. Spend some time reflecting on who you are becoming as an individual and where you can make the largest difference. "And he said to them, 'Go into all the world and proclaim the gospel to the whole creation'" (Mark 16:15 ESV).

Step Up to the Plate

What is one thing you can do today to make God smile? "Therefore I urge you, brethren, by the mercies of God, to present your bodies a living and holy sacrifice, acceptable to God, which is your spiritual service of worship" (Romans 12:1 NASB). God is pleased when you obey Him.

Even Clayton knows he must sharpen his skills on the mound if he is to stay on top of his game. Followers of Christ must do the same thing with their lives. There is always room for improvement.

DAY 5
TRUSTING GOD'S PLAN

Francisco Lindor
All-Star Shortstop
Cleveland Indians

By Beckie Lindsey

And we know that God causes everything to work together for the good of those who love God and are called according to his purpose for them.

—Romans 8:28 NLT

We find it easier to trust God when the sun is shining and we are winning the game. But when storm clouds roll in and we are no longer ahead on the scoreboard of life, our trust in God can plummet. The hard times are when we ask God why. We might be tempted to think God has forgotten us or doesn't care. Have you ever felt this way?

Francisco Lindor tells of such a time in his life, "Last year my sister went through cancer and treatments. She beat it, thank God for His help. There were those moments you want to question God and ask why. But at the same time, you have to realize His plan. You may not understand, and it's hard not to question. It's hard to leave it all with Him, but you have to."

Trust isn't easy to come by, and yet it's one of the most important and fundamental aspects of our relationship with

God. But before we can have trust in God, we must have *faith*, or belief in God. There are two aspects to faith: intellectual assent and trust.

Intellectual assent means believing something to be true. *Trust* is actually relying on the fact that something is true. Often a chair is used to illustrate this idea. Intellectual assent is recognizing a chair is indeed a chair. Trust is sitting in the chair.

Merriam-Webster defines trust as "assured reliance on the character, ability, strength, or truth of someone or something."

Interestingly, the Greek word for faith is *pistis*, which means trust.

God epitomizes these definitions. So, why is it hard to trust Him?

To believe *in* God is one thing. Many can believe intellectually with the historical facts that Jesus lived, died, and rose again. However, we cannot "see" Jesus atoning for our sins. This is where the trust aspect comes into play—when we put our faith in action by sitting in the chair.

You see, trust is built. Just like in our relationships with loved ones and friends, trust develops as we grow to know them better. When Francisco's sister fought cancer, this gave him the opportunity to put his faith in God into action by exercising trust in the Master's plan.

1. Replace negative thoughts with truth.
    When he found himself wrestling with God and asking why, Francisco relied upon the truth of God's Word and put it into action. "Everything you go through in life is for a reason. He's not just going to let you be by yourself at any point. You have to believe God and His Word. John 3:16

says it all. He loved us so much, so we should love him back with all our hearts. If I did not have faith and God in my life, I'd be in a bad place right now. I don't want to think about that." Instead of dwelling on the negative thoughts, Francisco reminds himself of the goodness, grace, and love of God by recalling Scripture. In doing this, he allows God to transform his mind: "And be not conformed to this world: but be ye transformed by the renewing of your mind, that ye may prove what is that good, and acceptable, and perfect, will of God" (Romans 12:2 KJV)

2. Surrender yourself and your trouble to God.

   "Life can be frustrating at times. God is in control, not me," Francisco says. "Some days will be harder than others. Some people will have harder struggles because there is no one to help guide them or coach them. That is when we need to rely on God. Just leave it with God, and He will take care of it. It doesn't mean you don't care, it just means you trust God to handle it." Francisco recognizes he is not in control and finds peace in his reliance upon God's control.

3. Pray to God for help with your challenges.

   "Don't ever feel alone. There will not be a burden in front of you that you will not be able to overcome with God's help. He will let you go through tough times for a reason: to make you stronger. He will help you with your challenges." Recognize God never leaves us alone. God desires to help those who cry out to Him.

4. Be patient for God to answer while you continue to pray.

   "Just be patient and wait. Keep on believing and keep on praying because it will all be okay. Always find ways to talk to God. It doesn't matter what time of day or night. He will be there. Whenever you can talk to God, it's always special and unique. I love to talk to God. I love to pray." Be persistent in prayer while you wait for God to answer. Even though it may feel as though you are doing nothing, prayer is doing something more powerful than you could do on your own.

On Deck

Be prepared for storms. The tempests of life do not discriminate—rich, poor, young, and old—we will all face hardships and trials at some point in our lives. Trust is the foundation of a healthy relationship with God. Just like building a home, our confidence must be built on a solid foundation that is deep enough to withstand the weight of the building and other stresses. In many ways, our lives are like buildings with solid bases. What is your foundation made of—doubt or trust? It's up to you.

Step Up to the Plate

Expect to put your trust in action. As Francisco says, God will let you go through things to make you stronger. God will allow us to go through situations in life to build our faith and trust muscles. This is not to be cruel. God is a great coach who knows how to bring out the best in us. As we become stronger, not only are we able to endure, but we will be able to help others face their storms too.

Can you identify any storms God used to minister to others or to further His kingdom? Are you in a difficult situation right now?

Look for ways God wants you to build your trust in Him. Fight the urge to quit by staying in the game even when you're down, confident in the assurance that God is right beside you.

Those who know your name trust in you, for you, O Lord, do not abandon those who search for you.

—Psalm 9:10 NLT

DAY 6
PROCLAIM YOUR SALVATION

Aaron Judge
Outfielder
New York Yankees

By Del Duduit

And this gospel of the kingdom will be preached in the whole world as a testimony to all nations, and then the end will come.

—Matthew 24:14

"The Lord has put me on this great platform, and I want to use it the right way," Aaron Judge told me before a game in Cleveland in late summer 2017. We spoke about social media and why he chooses to use it to be open about his faith.

Aaron's Twitter page sends a crystal-clear message. When you look at his account profile as of the time this book was written, you would have no doubt where he stands. It reads, "Christian. Faith, Family, then baseball." His picture displays 2 Corinthians 5:7, "For we walk by faith, not by sight" (NKJV).

More than 300,000 people follow Aaron's Twitter and are exposed to his solid testimony. He makes it obvious he is not ashamed of his Lord and Savior, and He wants the public to know he claims to be a Christian first and foremost.

Aaron grew up in a Christian home in California, and he was taught the right way. Still, he had to make his own decision to follow Christ, which he did at a young age, and has never looked back. He maintains a humble attitude and displays a readiness to help anyone, especially his teammates.

To him, his job with the winningest team in MLB history is a blessing and a way for him to tell the masses about the love of Jesus Christ.

"Any way I can spread the Word of God and get the message out there is a wonderful thing," he said. "I feel that is why I am where I am today."

People tend to listen to a man with Aaron's tremendous platform and stature—he stands six-feet, seven-inches tall and weighs 282 pounds. And while he isn't embarrassed to proclaim his faith, he does not throw it in anyone's face either. He wants the world to see Christ in him and read about his devotion to God.

"I just want to be able to inspire and encourage people," he said. "Any time you are able to share the Word of God and be a good example, then do it. That's how I feel, and that's what I try to do every day."

He realizes thousands of eyes are on him, but he doesn't mind the extra attention.

"Any time you can wear these pinstripes and play baseball for this team is a blessing," he said. "If I go 0-4 at the plate, it's still a great day for me because I play for the best organization in baseball, and I'm a child of the King."

Aaron displays an open faith, which helps him deal with the challenges he encounters. Although he looms larger than life to some young admirers, he has problems just like you and me.

But he serves a God who is much bigger than the mystique of the New York Yankees.

"I am so blessed right now that I am just enjoying life," he said. "I have a solid support team around me, and I serve a great God."

Aaron loves to play for the Yankees and loves to serve the Lord. While all aspects of life are fantastic for him right now, he expects he will run into trials. But he stays reassured the Lord will be there for him through the good times as well as the bad.

> If you stand before others and are willing to say you believe in me, then I will tell my Father in heaven that you belong to me.
>
> —Matthew 10:32 ERV

That is what life is about, Aaron added. "I want everyone to know Jesus Christ is my Savior, I have a tremendous family, and I play for the Yankees—in that order."

On Deck

Are you ready to tell the world you are a Christian? Perhaps you are in an environment where you might be punished if you display a Bible in your office. You might be in a situation where you sit at lunch with some coworkers who tell off-color jokes. Do you possess a desire to make a bold, spiritual profession and let others know you are a Christian? Do you find it hard to be a witness at times?

You are not alone. Once you make your stance public, people are given two choices—accept you or reject you. People in general long to be accepted in life. But there may come a time when you are forced to proclaim your position. Not many of us can be as tall or muscular or successful as Aaron, but you don't need an enormous physique or far-reaching platform for others to listen to you and respect your views.

Step Up to the Plate

Make it a priority to let the world know you are a Christian—the same way Aaron does. Here are some suggestions to send a clear message:

1. Be friendly to those you meet. Extend a kind word to whomever you meet wherever you meet them. A simple smile might invite folks to hear your testimony. And trust me, if you display an enthusiastic attitude, some people will be curious and ask why you are happy. Be prepared to tell them why. "In order that in the coming ages he might show the incomparable riches of his grace, expressed in his kindness to us in Christ Jesus" (Ephesians 2:7).
2. Engage those you meet. Once the ice has been broken, invite them to a church service or tell them about a special event. Show them you care about their soul.
3. Pray over your meals in public. This does not need to be a drawn-out prayer, but a simple bow of the head and a few words of thanks can be a great testimony.
4. Set a Bible on your desk at work, or hang a calendar with Scripture on it.
5. Wear a wristband with Scripture or a religious saying on it. These are popular, and you may even be asked what it stands for, giving you the opportunity to share how

gracious the Lord has been to you and how you always want to give Him praise.

6. Use social media like Aaron does. He puts his faith out there for everyone to see. Your tweets don't always have to be spiritual, but avoid posting anything that might be questionable or harm your reputation.

7. Have fun in what you do. Let others know you are a child of God and that you enjoy the way He blesses you in all of life's circumstances. "So I commend the enjoyment of life, because there is nothing better for a person under the sun than to eat and drink and be glad. Then joy will accompany them in their toil all the days of the life God has given them under the sun" (Ecclesiastes 8:15).

You may not have the enormous platform Aaron has, but rest assured there are eyes on you too. It may be your friends who watch you or someone in your church. It doesn't matter if you are at Yankee Stadium or a small grocery store. Demonstrate an indisputable witness for Christ, and make a difference wherever you are.

DAY 7
FOR THE GOOD OF THOSE WHO LOVE HIM

Andrew McCutchen
Outfielder
New York Yankees
Former NL MVP

By Ryan Farr

And we know that in all things God works for the good
of those who love him, who have been called according to
his purpose.

—Romans 8:28

Romans 8:28 is a verse with the comforting reminder that
in all things God is working on behalf of those who are his
children—in situations both big and small. This doesn't mean
the road will always be smooth and straight or that we won't get
a few bumps and bruises along the way. But it does promise we
serve a God who cares deeply about us, and He is committed
to working things together in such a way that we see transfor-
mation in our lives.

Not surprisingly, Romans 8:28 is the favorite verse of
Andrew McCutchen, an athlete who has seen God's direction
in both the peaks and valleys of his baseball career.

"Cutch," as he is known around the league and to a fan base
who has fallen in love with this likeable ballplayer, makes no

mistake about where he has placed his trust throughout his professional baseball career.

In high school, he was not only rated one of the top baseball prospects in the state of Florida, but he was also a phenomenal football player and track athlete. However, the career choice was simple for this man with a passion for the great American pastime, and in 2005, he was drafted eleventh overall by the Pittsburgh Pirates organization.

Like many other young prospects, he earned a living and a look from the majors while scrapping it out game-to-game in the minor leagues. He was unwavering in his pursuit of his ultimate dream and committed himself fully to the direction he sensed for his life. His persistence paid off as he was a South Atlantic League All-Star in 2006 and was named the Pittsburgh Pirates Minor League Player of the Year. But despite these accomplishments, he still remained in the minor leagues.

Though the circumstances were difficult, Andrew submitted himself to a God bigger than his disappointments. "Baseball in general has been a challenge," he said. "[God] helps in the midst of struggle and what I've been going through. On the field, sometimes, things don't go your way, but through Him, He gets my spirits in the right frame of mind."

In God's timing, Andrew realized his dream when he got called to the major leagues in 2009. Since then, his career has been filled with plenty of highs and even a few lows. From his selection to his fifth straight MLB All-Star Game in 2015 to his battle through the lowest batting average in his career in 2016, he has always acknowledged God has a plan for his life.

"The plan of God is the plan of God," he stated. "You have to trust in what He has planned for you—just continue that journey and keep on the road, stay positive, and find joy in the midst of the struggles."

The 2018 season threw Andrew another curveball after he was traded from the Pirates, a team he had hoped to remain on for the duration of his career, to the San Francisco Giants. Transition continued when he was later traded to the New York Yankees. But make no mistake, Cutch will be putting his head down and his eyes up again this season while he relies on God to transform an unexpected change into an unparalleled opportunity.

Perspective is everything, and his view of God's providence is clear. "I would not be here without Him. He has given me so many blessings and opportunities I don't deserve."

> But blessed is the one who trusts in the LORD, whose confidence is in him. They will be like a tree planted by the water that sends out its roots by the stream. It does not fear when heat comes; its leaves are always green. It has no worries in a year of drought and never fails to bear fruit.
> —Jeremiah 17:7–8

On Deck

Consider your life—where have you seen God's provision? When have difficult times made you question if God is truly leading? Throughout the Bible, we see examples of people who experienced the peaks and valleys of life and had the choice to either turn from God and His plan or surrender their fear and embrace what God had for them. Psalm 119 is a raw take on life from an individual's perspective. It's filled with reflections about the trials of life and why those who were not living right experienced abundance. However, through it all, the author of the psalm continually commits himself to God, His Word, and His plan. If you are discouraged by life's circumstances today or have ever grappled with how to be "real" in your interactions with the Lord, read Psalm 119, and reflect on what it means to have a godly heart while experiencing the victories and defeats of life.

Step Up to the Plate

How can you continually return to the realization we see in Romans 8:28, the reminder that God is always working together for our good? The best way is to have times of honest conversation with God like we see in Psalm 119. If this is something you find difficult or you don't know where to begin, consider the following.

How are you feeling? It is definitely okay to tell God your raw thoughts about a situation. Having a candid relationship with God means we tell him when we are confused by something that has happened. Maybe we don't understand why we have to go through a certain experience.

What might God be teaching you? Those who have played sports know one of the best teachers is adversity. Just because God allows us to go through difficulty doesn't mean He is against us or wants us to have problems. Often these times are the means God uses to shape us into the person He is calling us to be.

Make a statement of trust and reliance on God. In Psalm 119, the author takes a raw look at life. But then he recommits himself to God and His Word. Maybe you need to spend time being real with God about how you feel but also pledge to follow Him even when things are confusing or difficult.

Now watch and see how the Lord will direct your path and transform your heart through life's diverse experiences.

DAY 8
TELL THE TRUTH, NO MATTER WHAT

Andy Pettitte
Five-Time World Series Champion
ALCS MVP Pitcher
New York Yankees

By Del Duduit

Whoever conceals his transgressions will not prosper, but
he who confesses and forsakes them will obtain mercy.
—Proverbs 28:13 ESV

"I just needed to come clean with it," Andy Pettitte told me
in Tampa, Florida, during spring training at George M. Stein-
brenner Field in 2009. "I was having trouble sleeping at night."

He faced terrible scrutiny in 2007 when his name appeared
in the Mitchell Report with accusations he used Human
Growth Hormones (HGH). This led to a public apology, and
it badly damaged his spotless reputation. It also put in doubt
his consideration for entry into the MLB Hall of Fame. The
six-foot-five lefty from Baton Rouge, Louisiana, will be eligible
for the Hall of Fame in the 2019 class.

"Sometimes you feel you are living life as well as you can and
serving Him, and you feel like you are clicking, as far as your
walk is concerned," he said. "But you still get blindsided with
stuff. And you're like, 'God, what are You trying to do here?'"

The story began in 2002 when he contracted tendonitis in his left elbow. During his rehabilitation period, his trainer injected him with HGH, a synthetic hormone. It's meant to rapidly increase growth of muscle mass and help the body to heal. The MLB did not ban this non-steroid until 2005. However, some still considered it cheating.

For two days in 2002, he took HGH supplied by his trainer, and then he took it again in 2004. The second time, he obtained the drug through a prescription written to his father.

"It was during a time when nobody in the world would have known I did it," he said. "But I knew, my father knew, and my Lord knew."

Andy struggled whether to expose his father's involvement to the world. But deep down, it became clear. He must tell the truth.

"I didn't take it to get an edge," he said. "I took it to help my body heal. It was stupid on my part."

He told the facts, and later he used the experience to minister to young kids as his admission led to opportunities for him to talk at several churches about his career and how God helped him through his struggles. Telling the real story about what happened revealed God's grace even more to him.

"The Lord is always molding us and making us what He wants us to be," he said. "Things push you to speak more and share your testimony more, and I had the chance to do that."

He took a lot of heat, especially from the New York media. But ultimately people admired him for it.

His stint in the major leagues speaks for itself. Andy achieved a total of 256 career wins and 163 losses. He posted an ERA of 3.85 and earned five World Series rings with the Yankees. He won the American League Championship Series MVP with the Yankees in 2001 and made the All-Star roster three times.

Even when it hurt his reputation, showing honesty gave him the same rush as striking out the side in a bottom-of-the-ninth inning to win the title.

> Therefore, having put away falsehood, let each one of you speak the truth with his neighbor, for we are members one of another.
> —Ephesians 4:25 ESV

On Deck

Maybe you are facing a similar situation. Although the entire sports world may not be watching you, the Lord knows. Honesty might lead to disciplinary action at work or to a failing grade from a teacher. But cheating and getting by with falsehoods will only hurt you and your loved ones in the end. It's not worth it. Prepare yourself daily to be honest, even when it's not popular. This doesn't mean you must go out and intentionally hurt people either. You can appreciate the difference. It's about right and wrong and our conscious.

Step Up to the Plate

The hardest part in revealing the facts is worrying about the consequences. There may be serious repercussions, perhaps a relationship break-up or a job loss. But it's best to get them out in the open because keeping secrets can cause health problems. Andy had trouble sleeping at night. God already knows the truth, so you may as well come clean and break free of the burden of hidden sin on your conscious. If you are having trouble being honest, try the following:

1. Have the conversation. Although a tough first move, it must start somewhere. Inform people ahead of time—don't catch them off guard. Pray about it, and ask the Lord to give you the courage to speak. Choosing integrity proves to always be the right decision and will lead to an open and honest discussion. Having the talk might be scary at first, but use kind language, and show empathy and remorse. Handle it with the grace God provides.

2. Make sure the setting fits the significance of your topic. Less serious talks might take place in public, but a more important conversation might be best to take place in a small café or a park or even during a stroll. Be thankful you are not required to talk about it the way Andy did—in front of a podium and national television cameras.

3. Initiate the conversation and be positive. Say what you like about the individual. Try to stay upbeat, and see the good in the situation.

4. Caution the other person this might be difficult to say or hear. There are times hearing the facts may be tougher than revealing them.

5. Get to the point. Do not beat around the bush and sugarcoat it. Putting the conversation off makes it harder to state the truth. It gets easier after you ask for forgiveness and receive it.

6. Learn from your mistake. "God has taught me to do the right thing, no matter what," Andy said. Treat people the right way, and it will come back to you later in life.

7. Never hold a grudge, and forgive others if you are wronged. Ask those you wrong to forgive you.

8. Seek God's advice and pray. The devil will never tell you to pray; he wants you to lie. Always remember that. God will never approve a falsehood. "And this is the confidence that we have toward him, that if we ask anything according to his will he hears us" (1 John 5:14 ESV).

Integrity must be a part of the Christian journey. This doesn't mean to blab everything you know; use discretion and discernment. Lying lips are an abomination to the Lord. Those who tell the truth are His delight, and there are many benefits in pleasing God.

DAY 9
FIND A WAY TO SPREAD THE GOSPEL

Michael Lorenzen
Pitcher
Cincinnati Reds

By Del Duduit

> He said to them, "Go into all the world and preach the gospel to all creation."
>
> —Mark 16:15

"I kept hearing his words and couldn't get away from them," Michael Lorenzen told me. "I couldn't sleep because his words were just there in my mind. Over and over and over."

Michael was a junior baseball star at Fullerton Union High School in Southern California. He displayed a confidence in life and on the field and dreamed of the day he would play in the big leagues. He had many friends due to his stardom and personality. However, without any real church influence or positive role models in his life, he turned to drugs and alcohol.

His life changed forever on homecoming night. He and his buddies headed to one of their favorite hangouts on the Huntington Beach Pier. Amidst their fun, they noticed an older man they had never seen before. They edged closer and listened to what he had to say. The stranger grabbed his attention, and Michael stayed and listened.

The words were about Jesus and how the Lord would save Michael if he asked.

His friends ridiculed the preacher who approached the group and asked if he could share the story of Christ with them.

Although Michael was high on drugs, he remembered the story about a man who died for his sins. The story about how the Savior was crucified on the Cross and rose three days later echoed in his mind.

"I got convicted right there," he said. "I was high, but I knew right from wrong. I knew what I was doing was wrong, and I needed to change my life."

The friends soon left the pier and headed home. No one talked about the man who preached the gospel. They wanted to get away and have fun.

But the words about the Savior stayed with him. "Until then, I'd had a false sense about God," he said. "We didn't talk about it with each other that night—I just kept it all in."

A few days later, he and his brother attended Calvary Chapel Costa Mesa. Michael was miserable and knew what to do. He asked God to save him and turned his life around.

"I don't know who that man was, but he told me the truth," he said. "He had the courage to tell me and my friends about Jesus. I'll always admire that man."

After he gave his life to the Lord, he felt more alive and did not carry the burden of sin on his broad shoulders. He improved as a player, and coaches selected him to the all-state baseball team. He opted for college and played at California State University, Fullerton. In 2013, the Cincinnati Reds chose him in the first round.

Today Michael remains motivated to tell everyone he meets about his relationship with Jesus Christ. He likes to talk about how his life was headed in the wrong direction until he became a Christian.

"There are days when you don't feel like telling people," he said. "But I have to. I have to tell people what the Lord did for me. I just think about the man who told me, and it motivates me."

> However, I consider my life worth nothing to me; my only aim is to finish the race and complete the task the Lord Jesus has given me—the task of testifying to the good news of God's grace.
>
> —Acts 20:24

On Deck

Do your friends need Christ? Do you want to tell them about the Word of God? This may be a challenge, but we are all called to share the good news of Christ. Consider Michael's situation. Where would he be if a stranger had not talked to him about the Lord? He might have continued on a path with drugs and alcohol and ended a baseball career filled with promise, or even his life. Sharing the story of Christ can be a wonderful experience. You don't have to be a preacher to share the Word of God. And it doesn't take much time either. Michael's time with the stranger was short-lived, but it changed his life. A simple word can leave an impact, but actions can speak louder than words. Don't do something that puts your reputation in doubt and hurts your ability to be a witness.

Step Up to the Plate

If you have never witnessed to anyone, don't feel ashamed. But make the change in your personality now. There are some subtle ways to let others know you are a follower of Christ. Try some of these suggestions:

1. Keep a Bible in your backpack, office, or other area where you work. This might open the door for you to tell people it belongs to you and you read it every day.
2. Display a Christian decoration inside or on the outside of your car or locker. Some have put subtle Scriptures on their vehicles. Others will notice.
3. Utilize social media. This is a productive way to make your friends aware of where you stand. You can post Scripture and videos about your faith. You don't have to come across as an overbearing preacher, but you can let all of your friends know your views. This can be a wonderful way to meet new friends and open a discussion that allows you to share your story.
4. Send Christian holiday cards. They can also be cards for birthdays and other special occasions. There are many cards with Bible verses on them. You can send a best wish and a Christian message at the same time.
5. Pray over your meals at work, school, or in restaurants. This does not have to be a loud and long prayer or a public demonstration. A lowly bow of the head and a humble prayer in a few seconds can send a powerful message. Wait staff or those around you may notice and appreciate your gratitude.

6. Personalize your email signature. Instead of your name at the bottom, put a caption after your name. For instance: "John Doe, Blessed by God." You don't have to be pushy, but you can make your point in a subtle way.

7. Carry gospel tracts. These are a timeless way to share the story of Christ. You can hand these booklets out to any of your friends or to people you do not know. Most folks like free items, and these are perfect. Often tracts are simple and to the point but contain a clever message.

8. Be purposeful with your text messages. These are great ways to send Scripture to your friends. You can invite others to a church service or send a word of encouragement. When you are positive, you will seldom receive a negative response.

The harvest is plentiful but the workers are few. Ask the Lord of the harvest, therefore, to send out workers into his harvest field.

—Matthew 9:37–38

These are some tips to make you feel comfortable when you spread the Word of God. Not everyone can be a preacher or minister, but we are all called to tell others. Find a way to convey the message, "Jesus saves." Who knows what life you can impact for the kingdom. You might be the right person in the right place to tell the right story at the right time.

DAY 10
BREAKING A SLUMP

Tony Graffanino
Second Baseman
Atlanta Braves

By Scott McCausey

But he said, "Oh, my Lord, please send someone else."
—Exodus 4:13 ESV

Every muscle in Tony Graffanino's lower back and legs screamed in agony as he tried to stretch before the game. Fighting through aches and pains was the life of a ballplayer. Pitching arms resembled wet noodles, and nagging hamstrings stayed tight. Tony was trying to recuperate from a ruptured disc surgery, and his lower-back nemesis burned. He had taken for granted the skill required to twist his upper body at the plate or to pivot at second base while turning a double play. Now all those motions caused searing pain.

He wasn't one to complain, but his coaches and teammates on the Richmond Braves, an Atlanta farm team, took note of his performance. His .190 batting average and low power numbers were evidence that something was wrong. The season-long slump was hurting the team and the organization.

While Tony attempted to stretch the nagging muscles, Grady Little, the manager of the Richmond Braves, approached him.

"You know what, Tony? You never know how many ships are going to come in during your life. Your ship has just left the port."

Many times, our trek up the ladder of success is met with broken rungs. Honest opinions from people we respect cause us to miss a step. We try to explain ourselves and justify our actions, but we know excuses won't get us anywhere. When we are dejected and hurt, what do we do about it?

Coach Little continued, "The big club (Atlanta Braves) keeps calling about you, but I have to tell them you ain't ready."

Tony didn't know what to say. The thought never occurred to him the parent club wanted to bring him up in the midst of this slump. He did not want to disappoint them, so he worked out a plan with the coach. The disc in his back was not yet healing, and trying to play through it was only damaging his future. He shut down for the rest of the season to work on rehabilitating his injury.

Slumps affect all of us. We know we have the skills to get the job done, yet injuries, mental blocks, and maybe even fear keep us from the potential only we can reach. God met Moses in a fiery bush, but what really scared Moses the most were his job assignments.

God said, "Go tell Pharaoh what to do." Moses replied, "Who, me?"

God said, "Tell them 'I Am' sent you." Moses retorted, "Seriously, they won't believe me."

God said, "Here, take this staff. It'll turn into a snake, then reveal my plan." Moses said, "Yeah, but I can't talk very well."

God said, "Yes, you can." Moses said, "Send someone else."

Rather than follow the Almighty's instructions directly from the bush, Moses decided to remain in the slump. Sure, running from the problem is an answer, but it is not one that honors Christ, nor does it make Him proud. And what does hiding in a corner do for our self-confidence or our witness to the world? What is God's response to our defiance and cowardice?

> Then the anger of the LORD was kindled against Moses.
> —Exodus 4:14 ESV

Kindling God's anger is not a good idea. God's vengeance is described throughout Scripture with words like *avenging*, *wrathful*, and *flaming fire*. Moses finally got the hint. He stepped to the plate, swung his mighty Louisville Slugger, and watched as the water turned to blood, frogs hopped from the banks, and gnats formed from the dust of the earth. The slump was over.

Tony thought he could whip his back problems. He tried to tough it out a little longer but realized the best course of action was to take off for the rest of the season. He took some time to rest and began the arduous task of rehabilitating and strengthening his muscles. He returned to spring training and didn't make the big league roster, but he made the best of his time in Richmond. His call up was games away, and the slump was broken.

"Obviously if you go through a back surgery, you don't know if you'll ever be healthy enough to play again," Tony recalled. "That off season in '96 was huge for me just to get my injury corrected. I was able to inventory where I was and where I needed to be both mentally and physically."

On Deck

In the movie *For the Love of the Game,* the main character was a pitcher named Billy Chapel (played by Kevin Costner). Billy's goal was to clear his mind of all distractions before he threw the first pitch of a game. He tuned out the cheering and jeering crowd and ultimately pitched a perfect game.

Moses had to tune out the grumbling of the people and his own negative thoughts to focus on the task given him. Tony's nagging injury prevented an All-Star performance. Clearing our mind can prioritize the task at hand, while optimism and an understanding of God's desire for our lives can break the slump.

Step Up to the Plate

Gaining an advantage at the plate can be the result of research and study. Hitters and pitchers often receive detailed accounts of each other's tendencies. If the hitter knows a pitcher throws fastballs 85 percent of the time when facing a 3-2 count, he can dig in and wait for that pitch. Likewise, if a pitcher knows the batter never swings at the first pitch, he can simply groove a strike to get ahead in the count.

Understanding tendencies of the opposition can help to avoid a slump. Stay aware of the pitch count, how many outs there are, and where the defense is positioned. These can help gain advantages.

Another way to know the count is to understand our strengths and weaknesses. If we know we are weak at hitting the curve ball, we can work toward correcting that problem.

Knowing our limitations can also help avoid a slump. If we are tired, we should rest. If we're hurt, attempting to fight through the pain isn't always the best option. Tony learned this lesson, and it cost him an entire season.

If you find yourself in the midst of a slump, don't place blame, and don't continue to avoid the trial or hope someone else will step up and do what has been entrusted to you. "And I am sure of this, that he who began a good work in you will bring it to completion at the day of Jesus Christ" (Philippians 1:6 ESV). Dig in to the plate, keep your eye on the ball, and knock it out of the park. The end of your slump is one swing away.

DAY 11
THE STRUGGLE WITH SIN

R. A. Dickey
Pitcher
Atlanta Braves
Cy Young Award Winner

By Cyle Young

Count it all joy, my brothers, when you meet trials of various kinds, for you know that the testing of your faith produces steadfastness. And let steadfastness have its full effect, that you may be perfect and complete, lacking in nothing.

—James 1:2–4 ESV

Cy Young award-winning pitcher R. A. Dickey is the only MLB pitcher in history to record five consecutive games with no earned runs while still throwing over eight strikeouts in each game. A Nashville, Tennessee, native, the Texas Rangers drafted him out of the University of Tennessee in 1996. He would go on to play for six different Major League Baseball clubs: the Texas Rangers, Seattle Mariners, Minnesota Twins, New York Mets, Toronto Blue Jays, and Atlanta Braves.

His career spanned twenty-two seasons and had its ups and downs. In 2012, Dickey posted his best year when he won twenty games and posted a 2.76 ERA. That same year, he made the All-Star team and led the National League with 230 strikeouts.

As amazing as the 2012 season was for him, his career didn't start with the greatest of news.

In 1996, the Texas Rangers team physician discovered R. A. had a missing ligament in his right elbow. The team reduced his signing bonus from $825,000 to a mere $75,000, on worries Dickey wouldn't pan out in the MLB. He wouldn't let this challenge deter him from having a long career. His signature pitch was a knuckleball, and he decided if he wanted to have a long career, he needed to work hard to develop the perfect knuckleball. For the first twelve years, Dickey bounced between a few different clubs and minor league affiliates until the knuckleballer achieved a spot in the Minnesota Twins' starting rotation in 2009.

R. A. had several obstacles in his twenty-two years of playing professional baseball, but when asked to name his biggest one, he responded, "Sin is my biggest challenge. I fight it daily, like any other man." He speaks on the topic of sin with humble wisdom, "We have to battle against it every day. There is a lot of spiritual warfare going on every day against our faith. The devil would love to see us fall and destroy us; that's why we have to stay spiritually invested." He has devoted his life to Jesus Christ, but he still struggles to overcome the challenges sin presents. "I'm going to stumble here or there, like everyone else does. But when that happens, I stand tall, and I'm open and honest about it when I do."

Even though he is a professional baseball player, he knows he's not perfect. He knows there is a bigger cosmic struggle going on around him. He can stand firm knowing "the Lord will help, and He will always win."

The best advice this knuckleballer can give to someone when confronted with the challenge of sin is to know, "Running never solves anything. God knows where you are. Just stay in the Word and fight sin."

> Be on your guard; stand firm in the faith; be courageous; be strong. Do everything in love.
> —1 Corinthians 16:13–14

On Deck

Sin is the greatest challenge any person will face in this life. It is such a difficult thing to overcome that God had to send His own Son in the world to give you the ability to overcome sin once and for all through Jesus Christ's sacrifice on the Cross. You can't fight the battle alone, and you shouldn't try. God not only knows who you are, He knows where you are, and He knows your struggles.

Step Up to the Plate

Is overcoming sin a challenge for you? Do you struggle with making the right choices that honor God and His Word? You don't have to put the work in alone. You can take the following steps to overcome sin and temptation in your life.

1. Desire to defeat sin. You must first want to rid yourself of the wrong in your life. Pray for God to give you a desire to make the right choices, and ask Him to grant you the willpower to do so in difficult times and situations.
2. Identify the sins you need to defeat. Before you can conquer a sin, you first need to identify it. What is the root of the sin or temptation that is causing you to struggle?

Is this a habitual sin or a sin of convenience? Once you know what the sin is you are trying to overcome, you will be better equipped to find the biblical remedy.

3. Study the Bible's response to that sin. The Bible is God's guidebook for life. It doesn't specifically list *every* single sin known to man, but the framework and themes are contained within Scripture to help you govern every thought, action, and deed. Read and memorize Bible verses that can help you in moments of weakness and temptation. When Jesus was coaxed by the devil, he turned to Scripture for His defense. You can and should do the same when you are being confronted by sin in your life.

4. Choose the right way. This part is up to you. Don't give in to sin. Don't allow temptation to pull you in. Stand strong on the gospel and have self-control over your actions and choices. Trust in God's Word, and make the choice to refrain from sin. When you do, God is glorified. "The steps of a man are established by the LORD, when he delights in his way" (Psalm 37:23 ESV).

5. Don't give up. At times, you are going to fail. Sin and temptation will creep up in your life. In a weak moment, you may give in to the sin, but don't let that choice defeat you or break your spirit. As R. A. Dickey advised, be open and honest. Find someone to share with who can love you and encourage you to continue on for the Lord.

Keep the determination R. A. showed, and persevere through difficult times. All you need to know is that you play for the winning team. There will be struggles and battles with sin. But in those dark times, rely on your relationship with the Master to see you through.

DAY 12
LEARN FROM MISTAKES

Mike Sarbaugh
Third Base Coach
Cleveland Indians

By Del Duduit

> For the righteous falls seven times and rises again, but the wicked stumble in times of calamity.
> —Proverbs 24:16 ESV

"When you have some tough times, you need to lean on God more," Mike Sarbaugh said. "He's always there for us; we are the ones who stray away. We must recognize that and stay close to Him, even if at times we think we can't feel Him."

As a third base coach for the Cleveland Indians, Mike has to make a split-second decision—whether to send a runner home or hold him at third. Sometimes the choice can win or lose a game.

"You just have to recognize the situation and rely on your gut and from research you do on players," he said. "You have to know the arm strength of an outfielder—if he can make the throw to home—and I have to know our players and how fast they are. Plus, I have to be aware of the situation at the moment."

If the runner scores, he made the right call. If it turns out the other way, then Mike takes responsibility, and he capitalizes on the opportunity to learn.

"Sometimes I make mistakes," he said. "Once that decision has been made, I can't go back and redo it. I have to live with the outcome."

The same is true in our daily walk. We are faced with hundreds of choices each day. We decide what to wear, what to eat, and what to do while we work or are at school. These are part of our normal lives.

There are times you may not even be aware you made the right choice. For instance, you may take a different route to work and not realize an accident awaited you in the other direction. God took care of you, but you were spared the details.

You may choose to say something positive and brighten a person's day. It may not seem like a big deal to you, but it might bring healing to someone who lives with a silent hurt.

We take choices for granted since they are part of our lives and they become a routine. But when you make the wrong call, it can have a costly outcome.

We need to be reminded of God's grace and sacrifice so it will remain in our thoughts throughout our day. This can be especially difficult if you are away from your family for long periods of time, a challenge for professional athletes and coaches.

"In this game of baseball, we are gone from our loved ones a lot," Mike said. "Each day is a new one, and there are going to be some tough days when you are not home and wish you could be."

Grace and faith play an important role in order to avoid mistakes. Mike is blessed with a wife who supports his career and its many road trips. He appreciates the time home after time away.

"When I get back from being gone for a few days, I really put the emphasis on my family," he said. "They get my attention when I come through the door."

"My faith keeps me grounded," he added. "I just have been able to focus on what is important to me and have maintained that focus. And for me, my faith drives that."

It's important to maintain a laser-like focus on what's important to help deter you from a mistake. Mike's successful career as a coach began in 1995 when the Kingston Indians hired him as their hitting instructor. In 2009, he became manager for the Columbus Clippers and led them to victory in the 2010 and 2011 Triple-A championships.

Instructing is a way of life for him—he leads by example for some of the younger players who come into the major leagues.

"Some of these kids have never been in the public eye before or made the kind of money some make," he said. "I try to talk with them and put them in contact with players who can be a good influence for them. The last thing we want to see is a kid make a huge mistake."

Once this happens, the consequences can devastate and hurt a loved one or ruin a career. A reputation takes years to build and only seconds to destroy.

"We have to keep these kids focused on their job," he said. "I must be a godly example and help them. I like to plant that seed and watch it grow."

He stores up sound wisdom for the upright; he is a shield to those who walk in integrity.

—Proverbs 2:7 ESV

On Deck

You might be confronted with a tough decision. We all have been there. Now it's crunch time, and the clock ticks away. You may be thrown into a set of circumstances that requires you to make a choice. You may deal with temptation, such as money or covetousness. Deep down you know the right thing to do, but you experience trouble because you let the devil sit on your shoulder and argue. This is a tough time, and it's easy to give in—and the devil won't show you the result until it's too late.

Step Up to the Plate

It's go time. You must make a choice—what will it be? How will you make it? Pastor Rick Warren offers six tips to make a decision based on biblical principles.

1. Pray for guidance. Try to get God's take on the issue.
2. Get the facts. Do your homework to acquire as much information as possible—good and bad.
3. Ask for advice. Talk to a friend who went through a similar experience. What did they do, and what was the outcome?
4. Calculate the cost. This does not mean only monetary costs. For every action, there is a reaction. Try to plan ahead for what could happen in the long run.
5. Be prepared. Possess faith and expect great outcomes.
6. Face your fears. God uses the right person for the right job, although you may entertain doubts. God will never put you in a position He cannot handle. "The Lord is on my side; I will not fear. What can man do to me?" (Psalm 118:6 ESV).

"We don't always do the right things, but we have to try," Mike said. "If you have to hide when you do something, chances are you should not be doing it." Doing what's right can be difficult at times. But you will see positive results. Don't put your own needs at the forefront. For example, if you are offered a fantastic job but must move your children away from the friends and family they love, take that into consideration. Look at the entire picture of how it will affect those around you. After you have prayed and sought God's will, He will help you make a wise choice. Be aware of the arm strength of your opponent, and keep your eye on the third base coach when you head for home. If he sends you to the plate, go hard and avoid the tag. It's better to be safe than sorry.

DAY 13
RELATIONSHIP EVANGELISM

Adam Wainwright
Pitcher
St. Louis Cardinals
World Series Champion

By Cyle Young

But in your hearts revere Christ as Lord. Always be prepared to give an answer to everyone who asks you to give the reason for the hope that you have. But do this with gentleness and respect.

—1 Peter 3:15

In the last eighteen seasons of Adam Wainwright's pitching career, he has thrown 1,598 strikeouts and won 147 games. Three times he's been selected to the All-Star team, and he's won two Golden Glove awards.

A Georgia boy, Adam was raised in the church. He always went along with his mother and brother. But he confessed, like so many other people who have the same story, "I wasn't a full-fledged believer. I was not necessarily a nonbeliever. I was a skeptic."

In 2000, Adam met his new Gulf Coast League roommate, Braves pitcher Blaine Boyer. The teammates hit it off. They shared a deeper connection beyond just baseball. They shared a similar religious upbringing. But Blaine was much further along in his relationship with Jesus.

"I had a lot of questions for Blaine," he shared, "and there were a lot of arguments from my side, based on what he was trying to tell me."

Adam knew a lot about Scripture and all the Bible stories. "I just didn't know if Jesus was the only way," he admitted. A couple years passed before he began to break out of his stubbornness. He spent this span arguing the ultimate truth of the gospel before the Lord finally tapped him on the shoulder and persuaded him to attend the Pro Athletes Outreach (PAO).

Steve Hammond, the agent for both players, had encouraged him to go for years, so Adam made a deal with Blaine. He would go to the outreach, but if what they shared there couldn't convince him, they would relax and leave him alone about his spirituality.

That night, it all made sense. He was finally ready to listen. He had been hearing about Jesus for years, but he had never allowed himself to receive the words.

He professed, "I finally heard that this thing called Christianity is supposed to be a relationship with the Lord. It sunk in, and I became a believer and turned my life over to Christ."

His road to a vibrant relationship with Jesus started with his family and home church, but God used influential people like Blaine and Steve to assist him as he deepened his understanding of how he fit into God's overall story. He wasn't ready to make a decision for Christ when he was a child, but God waited patiently for the time to be right to welcome him into the family.

You never know how important a role you can play in someone's spiritual journey. God is always drawing people to him. Your task is to be prepared to love others and share the good news of Jesus whenever you can. Adam didn't expect his draft by the Braves in 2000 to be one of the key moments in his spiritual life. Every ballplayer is just excited to make it to the big leagues. But God had a different plan. He used other Christians to bring Adam to an eternity-changing decision through his association with baseball. If he can use MLB teammates, he can use people in your life too.

> Therefore, if anyone is in Christ, the new creation has come: The old has gone, the new is here!
>   —2 Corinthian 5:17

On Deck

Everyone needs a good Christian friend to walk with through life. Even professional baseball players have experienced the benefits of honest and genuine friendship. You can too. If you don't have a close friend in your life, reach out to find another believer who can stand in the gap for you and help you grow in your relationship with Jesus. If you have a strong walk with the Lord, you can also step up and be that kind of friend and mentor for others.

Step Up to the Plate

Have you ever found yourself in a similar situation as Adam, questioning whether Jesus is the only way to heaven? It can be difficult to wade through all the theories and opinions of the world around us. But like Adam, you don't have to figure it out alone. Good friends who love Jesus Christ can help you on your journey. If you want to experiences the same life-changing conversations and friendship as Adam and Blaine, you can follow these steps:

1. Have a hard conversation with yourself. Is something missing in your life? Is your relationship with Jesus where you want it to be?

2. Start regularly attending a church. Regular means every week. Allow yourself to be exposed to God's Word. Find a church you enjoy that feeds you spiritually, and get plugged in.

3. Find someone to talk to who already lives the Christian life you want to experience. You may have to step outside your comfort zone to connect, or you might ask a pastor to help you get connected.

4. When you get a spiritual mentor, ask hard questions, and be open to tough answers. No person will have all the solutions. And some of your questions won't have answers at all, but be real and allow your heart to hear from God.

5. Don't just hear the Word—listen and receive it. Open your heart to God and His Word. Don't bring in preconceived ideas or perceptions. Let your mind be a blank slate and allow the Holy Spirit to teach and equip you. "Consequently, faith comes from hearing the message, and the message is heard through the word about Christ" (Romans 10:17).

These steps aren't magical, but they will get you started. Adam experienced a life-changing relationship with Jesus Christ, and you can too. Christianity is all about relationships—with God and with each other. Be dedicated to creating bonds that spur each other onward, deeper into an understanding of God, His Word, and His ways.

DAY 14
SERVE THE LORD, NOT RELIGION

Brian Dozier
All-Star Second Baseman
Los Angeles Dodgers

By Del Duduit

Religion that God our Father accepts as pure and faultless is this: to look after orphans and widows in their distress and to keep oneself from being polluted by the world.

—James 1:27

In November 2013, Brian Dozier completed his second season with the Minnesota Twins, posting a batting average of .244 and blasting eighteen home runs. He planned to marry Renee and settle down to start a family.

A baseball season is long and tedious. Each team plays 162 games, not counting the post season.

"I love this job, but it certainly can take a toll on the body," he said. "I always like to relax for a few days after if I can and take it easy and rest."

Many players will take off for a soothing vacation once the season ends. Several head to the beach, a popular destination since their schedule usually ends in September.

But Brian felt a calling to do something else. Something important.

He had heard of Amigos for Christ, a mission group that takes trips to Nicaragua to help those in need.

This was perfect for him and his fiancé Renee.

"Instead of heading to the beach and sitting under an umbrella, we went on a mission trip for eight days," he said. "It turned out to the best experience of my life."

When he signed up for the trip, he did not tell anyone he was a professional athlete. He didn't want any special treatment or for people to cater to him. He traveled there for one reason—to promote the gospel of Christ.

However, his anonymity was short lived when some of the younger volunteers recognized him and began to talk baseball.

"When there is fantasy baseball out there, you can't hide," he said with a laugh. "But I stressed to everyone that I was no different from anyone else on the mission team."

When they landed in Nicaragua, some local residents greeted the mission team at the gate. Brian curiously asked one of them what religion he professed. The response surprised him.

"The man told me he didn't follow religion," he said. "I just follow Christ."

This brief conversation changed his life forever.

The thought process of being in love with the "idea" of serving Jesus Christ vanished. He served God and walked in faith, but there was a difference.

"That man helped me see that I had to be in love with *Christ* and not just the *concept* of Christ," he said.

His field of play moved from the diamond to the mission field. This meant hard work and no fancy clubhouses or expensive cars.

For a full week, Brian dug ditches to help create a much-needed clean-water system in a tiny village. Instead of swinging a bat, he used a shovel and pickaxe to dig a one thousand-foot-long, four-foot-deep ditch. He did this daily from 6 a.m. to 5 p. m. for eight days.

"We loved every minute," he said. "It went by so fast, and we all felt great at the end of each day. To look back at it, you'd think we would have been exhausted—and we were physically—but spiritually we grew stronger. That's why we loved it."

They loved it and returned the next year for their anniversary. "When you leave, you just feel good and feel the need to come back. So we did—we went back."

Baseball is a big deal in Central America. Once the people found out his identity, he brought back Twins gear—bats, gloves, and baseballs—to distribute.

He also had fun playing in a pick-up game the Amigos for Christ held with the locals during the trip.

"That week really, honestly changed my life," he said. "I've been a Christian and always tried to live right and do the right thing. But I really learned how to devote myself to Jesus Christ—and not just the religion."

Whoever oppresses the poor shows contempt for their Maker, but whoever is kind to the needy honors God.
> —Proverbs 14:31

On Deck

The best way to submerge yourself in the love of Christ is to be totally sold out for His cause. This does not always mean to quit your job and stand on a street corner preaching the Word. Find a cause and help. Give of yourself for the right reason. Don't do it for the fanfare or recognition.

Step Up to the Plate

It's your turn at bat. The team trails by one with a runner on second base in scoring position. Your team needs you to come through in a huge way with a base hit. Dig your spikes in and focus on the pitcher. Watch the ball, and in a split-second, decide if you are going to take a healthy cut or let it by and strike out.

You don't have to take a mission trip overseas to make an impact. There are many causes that might be closer than you realize. You could visit and help out at a boys' or girls' home or become active in Big Brothers Big Sisters.

But if you really feel God calling you to go on such a trip and you can't afford it, here are some simple things you can do to raise the resources.

1. Pray first and seek God's will. Research a mission organization thoroughly or talk to people who previously went on a mission trip. Finding the right Christ-led group is vital. You want this trip to be productive by accomplishing goals and making a difference.
2. Hold a yard sale and explain to people how the proceeds will be used. Post a sign to describe the trip. When people give to a cause, they appreciate information about what their money supports.
3. Write letters to friends and local churches asking for financial assistance.
4. Partner with friends to organize a car wash or bake sale in front of a popular spot.

5. Establish a GoFundMe account or use social media to draw awareness. Ask with humility, and don't be afraid of rejection. If you don't ask, you won't receive what you need.
6. Be a guest on a local radio program or submit an article to the newspaper to advertise what you are planning.
7. Ask friends to donate something to send with you such as Bibles. This might make them feel they are a part of the trip.

Blasting a home run over center field is a professional thrill for Brian. He's so good at it he participated in the Home Run Derby during the 2014 All-Star break. But he finds more personal satisfaction in digging a ditch in Central America. He would rather have a pickaxe and a shovel than a Louisville Slugger.

DAY 15
CONSISTENCY MAKES FOR A GREAT WITNESS

Cody Allen
Pitcher
Cleveland Indians

By Del Duduit

In everything set them an example by doing what is good.
In your teaching show integrity, seriousness and soundness
of speech that cannot be condemned, so that those who
oppose you may be ashamed because they have nothing
bad to say about us.

—Titus 2:7–8

Cody Allen always enjoyed the blessings of life and never took
anything for granted. He appreciated what he earned and kept
his lifestyle simple. He enjoyed time outdoors to hunt and fish.

But when he and his wife had their first child in June 2017,
his priorities shifted.

He didn't worry anymore about the issues that were out of
his control. The little things didn't matter, because now he had
bigger concerns.

His father had inspired him to be a strong man of character,
and he had always tried to follow his model. He made sure to
carry himself well and tried his best "not to mess up" in front
of fans who cheered him on when he pitched.

But now he has an even more important reason to be a strong witness.

"I have an actual person—a life—who depends on me," he said. "That is a tremendous responsibility." It's one he does not take lightly.

Cody desires to establish the same standards in his home that his father set for him. He is excited, dedicated, and ready to make adjustments.

"What was important to me takes a backseat," he said. "I want to be the best example I can be."

He is aware he must learn to show more patience and forgive often. He feels the eyes of his child on him every second he is home.

"I've got a little person watching me and expecting me to set the example," he said. "And I'm going to be exactly like my dad and get the job done."

For Cody, it's a matter of consistency.

Just like his job with the Indians, he must be ready to deliver when he is called upon out of the bullpen. And he has performed when asked.

In 2015, he pitched in seventy games and led the American League with fifty-eight games finished and thirty-four saves. He struck out ninety-nine batters and posted an ERA of 2.99 in sixty-nine innings. The next season, he played in sixty-eight innings and lowered his ERA to 2.51 in sixty-seven games.

His stats are consistent, and he knows his actions off the field must meet these same standards.

"It's about staying in the Word of God daily, challenging yourself and being honest with yourself."

Cody is strong enough to realize his possible weaknesses when he travels on the road with the team. Professional baseball players spend many nights away from their loved ones. But his faith keeps him grounded and in focus.

"That is when you need to grow as a man and as a Christian," he said. "When no one is around and you still do the right things, then that is the best judgment of character."

Jesus Christ the same yesterday, and to day, and for ever.
—Hebrews 13:8 KJV

On Deck

Maybe you can relate to Cody. We all can. He seems like the average guy who happens to be an MLB pitcher. He enjoys time to golf and eat chocolate chip pancakes. But now his family has expanded, and he has more responsibilities. There is a little person who depends on him for life. He knows one slipup can ruin a reputation and bring humiliation to his family's good name.

Maybe you act differently when you take business trips away from your loved ones. How you act when you are alone reveals who you are to yourself. If you pray and read your Bible at home, do you do it when no one else is around? When you have an opportunity to sneak out and do something you know is wrong, what choice do you make? Are you consistent, and do you set a good example everywhere you go? It might be easier for Cody since he is in the limelight with media watching close by. This might deter any thoughts he might have to do wrong as well. But Cody is grounded in the Word. Are you? Are you a consistent Christian example?

Step Up to the Plate

If you struggle with consistency in your relationship with the Lord, or if you want to become a stronger man of faith, try these suggestions:

1. Read and obey God's Word every day. There might be instances when you are challenged to find time to read the Word. Remove the obstacle and set a period in your day when it becomes your most important priority. Wake up fifteen minutes earlier or get off social media for a while.

2. Pray. I find it best to talk to the Lord after I read the Bible. I also chat with God while I'm in my car on the road at times. An active prayer life is essential to your daily Christian walk. If you can find time to have a discussion with your friends, then you can find time to talk to your Savior.

3. Attend church on a regular basis. Don't go once in a while or only on a religious holiday. Be an expected member of a church, and attend even when you don't feel like going.

4. Establish goals as a Christian. Read the Bible through in a year or make a certain number of hospital visits or witness to a person each month. Whatever you choose, make it your goal to be consistent as you work for Christ.

5. Serve others. After all, this is a trademark characteristic of a child of God. You could volunteer at a shelter or crisis pregnancy center once a month or take a mission trip. When you help people, it's a call to action. "For even the Son of Man did not come to be served, but to serve, and to give his life as a ransom for many" (Mark 10:45).

6. Stay focused on your reward. The ultimate destination for Christians is heaven. You must look beyond temptation and trials and find strength in Jesus Christ. If you do the first five steps, then this final one will come naturally.

7. Take on the responsibility and be consistent in your walk with God. Cody must always be ready to enter a game at any given time. You must also demonstrate the same attitude when it comes to your Christian journey. God will know it's your voice when you call upon Him for relief. Rest assured, He will close the deal, strike out the devil, and earn the win every time.

DAY 16
DREAM CHASERS

Jim Morris
Pitcher
Tampa Bay Devil Rays

By Scott McCausey

I will instruct you and teach you in the way you should go; I will counsel you with my eye upon you. Be not like a horse or a mule, without understanding, which must be curbed with bit and bridle, or it will not stay near you.
—Psalm 32:8–9 ESV

Coach Jim Morris studied the faces of the dozen or so boys signed up to play varsity baseball for the Reagan County Owls. After a short welcome speech, one of the players raised his hand. "Coach, we've only won one game the last three seasons. We have no idea why you took this job. People come though this town on their way to somewhere else."

Jim's own coaching staff shared this sentiment, "These kids are losers, and that's all they're going to be. There's nothing you can do about it."

These comments served as a challenge to the new coach. Jim had lived a life being told he was a loser since Little League. His dad's favorite saying was, "Kids are to be seen and not heard," and was one of the mantras that pushed him out of the house to use the gifts he had been given on the playing field. He played with kids twice his age, honing his skills in an attempt to make his dad proud. But at fifteen years old, he moved to his grandfather's house where he was given courage and learned about Jesus . . . and he pitched. He fired 85 mph fastballs for the Milwaukee Brewers and Chicago White Sox farm clubs, until his career was cut short due to arm surgeries.

God's Word mandates the importance of instructing youth in the game called life. Our Heavenly Coach supplies a playbook explaining conduct and rules. He gives us gifts to benefit the team and expects we will lead in a manner worthy of our calling. Imagine playing for Coach Jesus. Psalm 32 reminds us He is watching, and He's not going to force us as with a bridle in a horse's mouth. Our name is slotted on the lineup card, and we play hard for the benefit of the team.

The first game for the Owls was a doubleheader. Jim's team lost 15-1 and 15-2. Standing on home plate after the game, Jim offered a prayer, "God, what can I do to help these kids? How can I get through? How can I push them without breaking them? How can I get them to dream further than tomorrow?" The answer came quickly, "Go down there and tell them what your grandfather taught you, dummy."

He headed to the dugout, armed with a pep talk worthy of Casey Stengel. He told the kids about courage and hope, how to beat the odds and about living big dreams. Halfway through, his catcher interrupted. "Hey, coach. What about your dreams?"

He replied, "My dream is to watch you guys do great in the classroom, great on the field, go to college, and see what's out there. Make up your own mind about what it is you want to do."

His catcher retorted, "That's funny, because we all think you still want to play baseball."

Laughing at this response, "Nope. I do not. The doctor told me no. I've gained fifty pounds in ten years. The only place I run is to the refrigerator, and I look more like a scout than a player."

"But, coach," the reply was quick. "The way you teach us the game, you know how to act and react to everything. And when you throw batting practice, we can't hit it."

Jim was frustrated. "That's because you can't hit," he said.

The eighteen-year-old catcher spoke with wisdom above his years. "Why are you telling us to chase our dreams when you aren't willing to do it yourself? What if we start winning, coach? What if we win a district championship? Our school has never done that. Will you try out for the big leagues?"

Jim argued for twenty minutes and finally relented. "If you guys win a district championship, I'll find a tryout, and it's going to be embarrassing."

The coach didn't think a district title was possible. Yes, he could turn the program around. But win a title with a group of guys who just lost back-to-back games with a combined score of 30-3? Not likely. So they struck the deal. And the Owls began to win.

> Hear, my son, your father's instruction, and forsake not your mother's teaching.
>
> —Proverbs 1:8 ESV

On Deck

The bread and butter of a pitcher's repertoire is the fastball. It can be thrown a couple different ways. When the ball is gripped across the seams (a four-seamer), a straight ball is thrown, sometimes with a cutting action. When thrown with the seams (a two-seamer), a sinking action occurs.

The advantage of throwing the four-seamer is accuracy. A pitcher relies on the location of his fastball to throw strikes and get the advantage against the hitter. Believers rely on the unchanging ways of Jesus. Hebrews 13:8 tells us, "Jesus Christ is the same yesterday and today and forever." Since He remains the same from beginning to end, we can depend on His word, we can trust His instruction and counsel.

The two-seamer supplies deceptive movement. A high velocity pitch with this grip is like a curveball with power. When it's controlled, it's hard to hit. Jeremiah 29:11 (ESV) says, "For I know the plans I have for you, declares the LORD, plans for welfare and not for evil, to give you a future and a hope." When we couple the understanding of God's plan to receiving His instruction from Psalm 32, we accomplish great things for the kingdom.

Step Up to the Plate

Unlike sports, where a timer dictates the end of a game, baseball doesn't end until the last out is made. A team can be losing by a dozen runs and still have a chance to win. God's instruction tells us when we run the race with Jesus as the perfecter of our faith (Hebrews 12:1–2), we can come back from all our sin and still win. In baseball, anything is possible. In life, Jesus makes anything a reality.

The Owls kept winning to the tune of a district championship. Jim kept a promise and God worked a miracle. The Coach is cheering you on. Are you listening for the dreams He has for you?

DAY 17
98 MPH

Jim Morris
Pitcher
Tampa Bay Devil Rays

By Scott McCausey

For I know the plans I have for you, declares the LORD, plans
for welfare and not for evil, to give you a future and a hope.
—Jeremiah 29:11 ESV

Coach Gassaway looked up from his sign-in clipboard to the
shadow of a husky, middle-aged man in a softball uniform.
"How many kids did you bring to the tryout?"

Jim Morris looked down at his three children, "I only
brought these."

"No," Coach Gassaway shook his head. "How many to
actually try out?"

Indecision already enveloped Jim after an hour-plus drive.
He looked down at the major league scout. "I'm the coach for
the Reagan County Owls, and I'm here because of a promise.
You see, during a pep talk to my team after they dropped a
double header, I told them they were quitting life by not taking advantage of their skills and dreams. Halfway through my
inspirational speech, they interrupted and wondered why I was
squandering my opportunities, my dreams. They challenged

me to try out for the big leagues if they followed their aspirations and won districts."

Jeremiah the prophet wrote letters to the scattered Israelite leaders in captivity to remind them God had a plan. They weren't to simply settle among the pagans and adhere to their practices to fit in with the crowd. It is common practice today to avoid confrontation through acceptance. Rather than share an opinion from God's Word, no opinion is given, or worse yet, God is abandoned. God's dreams for his people are disregarded.

Jim could have easily broken the promise made to his players to try out. They would have been upset, but time would heal the deal. Yet he was a man of honor. God never broke a promise, and neither would he.

He continued, "My grandpa always taught me if you make a promise, you always live up to it, no matter how bad it turns out. If you can't live up to the promise, you don't make it. My players lived up to their end of the bargain, I'm here to do mine. You'll get a good laugh, just please let me throw so I can go home to tell my kids I did it."

Coach Gassaway said, "I'll let you throw, but you're going to throw last. These kids are here for serious business."

He signed his name on the clipboard and took a seat in the bleachers. Minutes turned into hours as teenagers were given their shots. He changed diapers, read books to his kids, and watched the field, wishing the day would end. After four and a half hours, his name was called. He grabbed his glove, gave instructions to his eight-year-old to watch his siblings, and headed to the mound.

Coach tossed him a ball. "How many pitches do you need to warm up?"

Jim sarcastically replied, "None to embarrass myself."

As the coach walked back to his position behind the back-stop, Jim stretched his arm. He thought to himself, "Work fast and get out of here. And don't forget the kids on the way out!"

The teen catcher crouched behind the plate and flashed the signal for a fastball. Jim gripped the ball and came to a stretch. He rocked and fired. The ball exited his hand in a white streak, whistling to the plate and popping the catcher's mitt. "That felt great and was a surefire strike," he thought as the catcher returned the ball.

He got set to throw the next pitch when he noticed the coach behind the screen shaking the radar gun. "Oh great," he thought. "I don't even throw hard enough to register a speed." As he continued to work, more coaches with radar guns showed up. "I'm either really bad, or something I'm doing is really good."

He finished throwing to the echo of his one-year-old crying from the stroller. He jogged to his kids and started loading up. He had fulfilled his promise.

"Hey, pitch," the catcher was running to see him. "That was some good throwing. You threw better than anybody today."

Jim joked, "Son, that's because no one else here could throw."

"No, you had 'em talking back there." Pointing to the coaches huddled behind the backstop. He reached out and shook his hand.

Not far behind the catcher was Coach Gassaway. "Jim, I remember you. Fifteen years ago, at Ranger Junior College, you were a football star that everyone wanted to make a pitcher of. I don't know what you've been doing these last few years other than eat," smiling and poking Jim's gut. "The first pitch you threw without warming up was 94 mph. Every pitch after that was recorded at 98 mph."

Jim couldn't believe what he heard. He reflected on what his kids told him and what they saw in him. God had something great in store, yet he was stuck in a cultural rut. He bought into the lies that a man in his midthirties couldn't accomplish great goals.

On Deck

Although it appeared he showed up at this tryout without any practice, truth be told, Jim pitched batting practice to his high school team day after day. Through this experience, his arm and body strengthened. It wasn't his goal to pitch at a higher level, but God had other plans. Jeremiah encouraged the leaders to live their lives knowing God was at work. He never leaves us and always strengthens us when we flex our spiritual muscles. Does your practice mimic your game performance?

Step Up to the Plate

A "jugs gun" is a sports radar gun that measures the speed of a pitch. However, this device is not always the barometer of success for a pitcher. Many scouts will tell you they look for pitchers who can throw a fastball in the nineties, but great control is the key. As believers in Jesus, we are to be in control of our actions and speech to enhance the kingdom. When we practice control, we win hearts for our Savior.

Coach Gassaway said, "Don't be surprised to get a phone call. They (the leaders in the Tampa Bay organization) are going to think I'm crazy, but if I don't call it in, you could sign with someone else, and I'll get fired."

He drove home in disbelief. And coach was correct. When he called to report what he and many other scouts witnessed, the front office hung up on him. He continued to share the story, and by the time Jim got home, the answering machine was filled with twelve calls wanting him to throw again. The details of his comeback were later dramatized in the movie *The Rookie,* made in 2002.

Practice like you play, and make dreams a reality.

DAY 18

BE A CONSISTENT ENCOURAGER

Albert Pujols
Multiple MVP Winner and First Baseman
Los Angeles Angels of Anaheim

By Del Duduit

These commandments that I give you today are to be on
your hearts. Impress them on you children. Talk about
them when you sit at home and when you walk along the
road, when you lie down and when you get up.
—Deuteronomy 6:6–7

"I have a great family and great friends who help me along the
way," Albert Pujols said. "I have a great pastor and great people
around me who support me."

Albert has been playing professional baseball since April
2001 when he made his debut with the St. Louis Cardinals.
The unanimous choice for Rookie of the Year went on to win a
truckload of awards, including three MVPs, two Gold Gloves,
six Silver Slugger Awards, and two World Series rings. He will
be considered a high favorite to be inducted into the Hall of
Fame on the first ballot after he retires.

There is nothing Albert has not won while playing in the
MLB. He's considered by many to be the perfect baseball

machine. His swing has been described as quick, quiet, and the same every time. He is a model of consistency at the plate.

Still, the ten-time All-Star needs support.

"Really, there is no easy way in this sport," he said. "I love this game, but it can be hard at times too. It's hard being away from your family so much, and hard to find time because there is such a demand on our time."

He is a fan favorite and enjoys spending time with his family when he is able. But he realizes he has a high-profile job as well. He has learned to take the good with the bad—although he has rarely seen the latter.

"You know, there are ups and downs in this game and in life," he said. "The beautiful thing is that this is just a game of baseball. I am not fighting for my life. I am playing baseball."

With that attitude, he tries to enjoy as much as he can while giving God all the glory—"In everything I do."

The Lord has blessed Albert and his family and has allowed him to use his platform as an MLB star to tell others about Christ.

"I am so unworthy of these blessings," he said. "But I recognize it, and I have been able to do a lot of things through this game. I use this wonderful opportunity to support my family and encourage everyone I meet."

In 2005, Albert and his wife Deidra launched the Pujols Family Foundation, which promotes awareness of Down syndrome and strives to support those who have it, along with their families.

"This is very near and dear to our hearts," he said. "It's a way to help and encourage and let everyone know there are people out there who care." He and his wife have five children, including Isabella, who was born with Down syndrome.

The charity also aids people who have other disabilities or life-threatening illnesses, as well as children and families living in impoverished conditions in the Dominican Republic. Albert has taken many trips to the Dominican Republic to provide supplies, and he has brought along doctors and dentists to those who need medical attention but cannot afford it.

"It's just a calling," he said. "We are all called by God to help everyone we can."

Everyone faces challenges in life. Just like one of Albert's favorite movies, *Facing the Giants*, we must all lean on the Lord to overcome obstacles. They are not put in our path to distract or punish but to teach us how to overcome and trust in Christ.

Someone is watching how you handle a situation. Be a godly example and try to raise other's spirits during times of trouble.

> But those who hope in the LORD will renew their strength. They will soar on wings like eagles; they will run and not grow weary, they will walk and not be faint.
>
> —Isaiah 40:31

On Deck

What challenges do you face? Maybe you are faced with a job loss or the death of a loved one. No matter the obstacle, be prepared to face it head on and not run. The devil wants you to take the convenient route and give up. He wants you to get angry with God and turn your back on Him. What will you do when a curveball is thrown at you?

Step Up to the Plate

You are faced with a circumstance you did not expect, but it's here, and the way you handle it can make or break your situation. Here are five ways to be an inspiration:

1. Practice stewardship. You don't need to be rich to be a good steward. Time is also a valuable commodity. Give yourself to others and show them how much you care. Put others first and embolden them. "Moreover, it is required of stewards that they be found faithful" (1 Corinthians 4:2 ESV).

2. Extend your friendship to others. If you demonstrate your willingness to help a stranger, the Lord will notice. Perhaps there is someone in your church or neighborhood you don't know well. Make it a point to get to know them and find out if they need help with anything.

3. Build partnerships. Join a prayer group or a civic organization. This will build strong alliances while you are doing something positive with your time.

4. Develop leadership skills. Organize a prayer group or work to raise money for an organization. Serve on the front lines. This will strengthen your devotion and raise you up as a leader who can encourage others.

5. Rebuild a relationship. Perhaps you, like many, have a relationship in need of repair. Take the first step and offer a friendly white flag. You are not on this earth long, and fighting is a waste of your valuable time. No matter the issue, bring a friend back to the fold. Forgiveness is a wonderful gift from God. "So in everything, do to others

what you would have them do to you, for this sums up
the Law and Prophets" (Matthew 7:12).

There is no question Albert is a leader on the field as well
a motivator. He didn't become one overnight. The power of
the Holy Spirit made him what he is today. One of the many
awards Albert received during his standout career in the MLB
was the Heart and Hustle Award in 2009. You too can inspire
others with your heart for God. Let Him take control of your
life so your light will shine and lift others up in this dark,
cruel world.

DAY 19
STOP WHAT YOU ARE DOING

Mike Matheny
Manager
St. Louis Cardinals

By Del Duduit

So, because you are lukewarm—neither hot nor cold—I am
about to spit you out of my mouth.

—Revelation 3:16

"We got hit over the head about being comfortable with the
act of being religious instead of having a personal relationship
with Jesus," Mike Matheny said of a visiting preacher years ago.
"It really sunk in, and I asked myself a lot of tough questions."

He was nine years old in Columbus, Ohio, when he heard
the message. He was raised in a Christian home and was always
exposed to that way of life. But it was in that service at Fellowship Baptist Church when something became clear to Mike.

He was lukewarm. He was going through the motions.
After he heard that message, he wanted more. He wanted to go
deeper in his relationship.

"I went to my parents, and they were wise enough to open
the Word of God," he said. "They went to the Book of Romans
and explained the need we have for the gospel."

He read that everyone has sinned and deserves death. But
through Christ, we can all have eternal life.

That hit Mike harder than a 95-mile-per-hour fastball.

He saw his need of the Savior in a different way. He no longer wanted to be lukewarm.

"At that point, my parents showed me the opportunity I had to have that relationship with Christ and to have my sins forgiven," he said. "At that point, I began my lifelong walk."

Mike has truly been blessed spiritually and professionally.

He played college baseball at the University of Michigan and was later drafted by the Milwaukee Brewers in 1991. He was one of the most durable and accomplished catchers of his era. He won four Rawlings Gold Glove Awards and set records in the MLB among catchers for the most games played without making an error (252). He is one of only three catchers in MLB history with an errorless season of at least one hundred games, and he set the single-season team record for the San Francisco Giants in fielding percentage in 2005 at .999.

Consistent concussion symptoms forced him to retire in 2007. Five years later, the Cardinals hired him as the team's manager, even though he had no professional coaching experience.

In 2015, he became the first manager in MLB history to lead his team to the playoffs in each of his first four seasons. In 2013, St. Louis won the National League pennant but lost to the Boston Red Sox in the World Series.

With all his success on the diamond, he still never went back to being lukewarm. He has never forgotten the sermon he heard that challenged him at a young age, and he wants to stay on fire for the Lord.

"We all make mistakes and have sinned," he said. "But there is only one way to be forgiven. Christ made the ultimate sacrifice for you and me, and we all have the opportunity to accept or reject Him."

He often reflects back on that day when he was nine years old and is thankful he made the right decision.

"I realized that was what I needed and wanted," he said. "No matter what your age is, you can have that personal relationship with the Lord."

He knew his decision to accept Jesus as his Savior was not about himself—but about *Him*.

"It's in no way about me," he said. "He will guide you through life."

Mike's Christian walk has been similar to his fielding percentage—nearly perfect. He has had struggles along the way like all of us do, but he keeps the ball in front of him and blocks the plate. He stays grounded in the Word of God and practices daily.

Teach me, and I will be silent; and show me how I have erred.
—Job 6:24 NASB

On Deck

Maybe spiritually, you are in a slump. Just like major league hitters, you must keep swinging. Consider changing up your routine. When some hitters are in a rut, they try different bats or do something else to mix things up. Players can't come out of a slump until they acknowledge they are in one. The same is true for Christians. Take spiritual inventory and ask yourself how long it has been since you truly worshipped the Lord.

Step up to the Plate

Perhaps you recognize you are lukewarm. Congratulations, because this is a big first step! Now what will you do about it?

According to one of my favorite lessons taught by Tom, my Sunday school teacher, all you need to do is STOP.

> **S—Serve others.** Nothing else will make you bigger in God's eyes than when you serve people with a humble heart. "Whoever brings blessings will be enriched, and one who waters will himself be watered" (Proverbs 11:25 ESV).
>
> **T—Trust in the Lord.** Get into God's Word and learn to put your faith in Him. At times when it seems hope might be lost or you are at a breaking point, look to God. When you flip a light switch, you trust the room will become bright. When you cross a bridge, you trust you will make it to the other side. God knows what He is doing, and His plan is always best. "Commit to the Lord whatever you do, and he will establish your plans" (Proverbs 16:3).
>
> **O—Obey.** As parents, we expect our children to do what we tell them. The Lord wants the same from you. Don't argue or fight—just do what He tells you even when you have doubts. He doesn't ask you to understand, only to obey. "Do not merely listen to the word, and so deceive yourselves. Do what it says" (James 1:22).
>
> **P—Praise.** This is the absolute best thing you can do. God wants us to give Him the glory for everything. When you are on your knees or when your arms are raised, it's a wonderful feeling. "God is spirit, and his worshipers must worship in the Spirit and in truth" (John 4:24).

STOP, and ask God to reignite your fire and break you out of your slump.

DAY 20
DO SOMETHING

Blaine Boyer
MLB Pitcher

By Del Duduit

> But Jesus said, "Let the little children come to me and do not
> hinder them, for to such belongs the kingdom of heaven."
> —Mathew 19:14 ESV

Has an event grabbed your attention and beckoned you to
become involved?

You see commercials of neglected and abused animals that
tug at your heartstrings. You are exposed to the needs of children who are ill and need your financial help. And you are
enlisted to help our wounded veterans. There are many more
examples, and most are worthy causes.

MLB pitcher Blaine Boyer, father of two, observed some
tragic events while overseas, and he received a divine call to do
something about what he had witnessed.

Remember the movie *Taken*?

The plot centers on human trafficking. The main character's
daughter and her friend are kidnapped in Paris and sold as sex
slaves. Liam Neeson plays a former CIA operative who goes
on a mission to bring his daughter back to the US alive and

eradicate the traffickers. There have been two sequels since the original in 2008.

This movie franchise capitalizes on a real-life scenario played out by Blaine and former MLB first-baseman Adam LaRoche who retired in 2015. The duo traveled together to Southeast Asia for ten days in 2016. This trip was not a vacation but a mission to help victims of human trafficking.

"Adam and I were thrown into a situation that changed our lives forever," he said. "It went from scary to fulfilling and everything in between—from confusion to jubilation. It wrecked us both."

The athletes' trip was sponsored by Exodus Road, an organization with a strategic focus on the fight against human trafficking. Their assignment was to go undercover and secretly record video inside the dark brothels in an effort to help stop the "business."

"When we came back to the states, we knew we had to be involved with this mission," Blaine said.

"It just ruined us," he added. "We were in some nasty situations. It broke our hearts, and now this is what the Lord has called us to do—fight for these people who have been stolen."

The pair found themselves in some sticky predicaments. One false move inside the brothels, and they could be killed. "We were in deep," Blaine said. "But that is why we were there—something needed to be done."

The focus of Blaine's prayers changed after this experience. "Lord, let me see people the way You see them. What breaks Your heart, let it break my heart too."

God answered. "I could hear the Lord telling me, 'This is what I have for you boys to do.'"

Adam now sits on the board of directors for DeliverFund, a group that works to equip law enforcement to arrest human traffickers. Both he and Blaine are now part of this nonprofit ministry.

> I will take my stand at my watchpost and station myself on the tower, and look out to see what he will say to me, and what I will answer concerning my complaint.
>
> —Habakkuk 2:1 ESV

On Deck

Has there been an event or circumstance that grabbed your attention, broken your heart, and beckoned you to get involved? Perhaps you know someone who suffers from the pain and hurt of an abortion. Maybe you are increasingly disheartened by those across the nation who seek to take away our religious freedoms and make Christians a target of ridicule and fodder. What can you do to make a difference?

Step Up to the Plate

Blaine and Adam said they felt God move them in the direction to help rescue children from sex trafficking. This is a noble yet dangerous undertaking, and people are needed to help. But not everyone is cut out for this line of work. But there may be other areas in which the Lord leads you to get involved. God has a plan for your life, and He expects you to find a way to spread the gospel. "He said to them, 'Go into all the world and preach the gospel to all creation'" (Mark 16:15).

Sitting on the bench is easy, especially when there is an ace on the mound who throws heat. This is your chance to tighten up your batting gloves, spread the pine tar on the bat, and dig your spikes into the dirt. Do something!

1. Educate yourself. There are many social issues in the world today. Examples include abortion, suicide, drug abuse and alcoholism, religious discrimination, animal abuse, sex trafficking, homelessness, euthanasia and assisted suicide, gang violence, and disease. Before you decide to become involved with a cause, get to know the facts, history, and circumstances. "How much better to get wisdom than gold! To get understanding is to be chosen rather than silver" (Proverbs 16:16 ESV).

2. Pray for an opportunity. Ask the Lord for guidance and a chance to work for a cause that will bring glory to His name. You have been chosen for a reason—follow His will for your life. When you are ready and the time is right, the Master will open the door for you to become a part of the team.

3. Be dedicated. If you join a cause, stick with it, and be ready for extra innings. If you show up for an event and only a few people are there, don't be discouraged. There is work to be done. Jump in and find out how you can help. "For where two or three are gathered in my name, there am I among them" (Matthew 18:20 ESV).

4. Be willing. Your job might be to walk in parades, work in a church bus ministry, serve food at the Salvation Army, or manage a social media account for a cause. Maybe God wants you to organize a home Bible study or run for

political office. Even if it's out of your comfort zone, God has selected you for a reason. Be assured He will not ask you to do what He does not equip you to do. "For you were called to freedom, brothers. Only do not use your freedom as an opportunity for the flesh, but through love serve one another" (Galatians 5:13 ESV).

Blaine said he and Adam's passion to fight human trafficking had to come from God. He said he could not get away from the calling, and he knows this mission is what the Lord wants him to do with his life. God's plan for you may not put your life in danger, but you can still get out on the front lines and make a difference. Find your ministry, and let the Savior guide you. Get off the bench and onto the diamond, and make the play everyone will remember.

DAY 21
PUTTING YOUR TRUST IN GOD

Mike Rikard
Vice President of Domestic Scouting
Boston Red Sox

By Del Duduit

It is better to trust in the LORD than to put confidence in man.
—Psalm 118:8 KJV

"Over the past ten years or so, I have prioritized my life and my faith," Mike Rikard told me. "I have put the Lord first in my life in all things, and He has allowed me to have peace and clarity in what I do."

Mike has a stressful, yet enjoyable career. He oversees the amateur draft for the Boston Red Sox and makes the recommended choices of players for the organization.

He has been with the Red Sox for the past sixteen years and loves what he does for the championship club. For the past few years, he has served as the director of scouting, which requires him to have a unique perspective of each position on the field and manage seventeen professional scouts and six cross checkers. Not an easy task.

"I deal with staff every day," he said. "Each one has a different personality, and eventually there is the inevitable drama that will exist on a staff of strong-willed, yet wonderful men."

Mike has learned how to deal with different characteristics in a positive way and has accepted the challenge to demonstrate his strong faith to others in a professional manner. He treats each person with respect and hopes his colleagues will notice and reciprocate. "In Luke, it tells us to treat others the way you want to be treated (Luke 6:31), and I honestly try to do that every day," he said.

But that is not the most stressful part of his job.

The historic franchise depends on him to make selections of new players for them each year. The organization relies on his judgment to improve the team. Many of the players selected in the draft will earn a high paycheck at a young age.

If the player does as well as expected, then Mike looks brilliant. If it goes the other way and the Red Sox pay a lot of money to a person who doesn't turn out to be as good as he thought, then Mike has to bear some of the responsibility for the pick.

"We basically put our future in the hands of these young players, and that can be very stressful," he said. "Through all this, I have learned to manage my faith and trust God more than ever."

Although the Bible instructs us not to worry as Christians, we are humans who struggle with the "things not seen" part.

To say you possess faith is one thing, but to *have faith* is another.

"It's a constant battle," Mike said. "We are all sinners, and we all get weak."

The difference, he added, is to treat each obstacle the best way possible and give it to the Lord.

"We know we can put it behind us," he said. "It's the same in life as it is in sports. That's the great thing about faith. We can leave it in God's hands and not worry about it. I'm trying to do that more and more."

He has learned to trust in God more over the past ten years. His job's unique challenges include frequent travel away from his wife and three children and long hours at the ballpark.

Each spring he tells them, "I'll see you in two weeks." But he has put God first on his priority list, and life seems to fall into place.

"It helps me have more space and allows me to do a better job," he said. "God has provided the balance for me to work and still be a father to my kids. I have an amazing wife, and we have made it work."

> Cast thy burden upon the LORD, and he shall sustain thee: he shall never suffer the righteous to be moved.
> —Psalm 55:22 KJV

On Deck

Do your extracurricular activities or your job take too much time away from your studies or your family? Or perhaps you own your own business or are supporting yourself through school and sense the pressure of making ends meet. Ask God to help you strike a healthy balance between getting your work done and maintaining a close relationship with God and those you love the most.

Step Up to the Plate

Your priorities show your true colors. While it is ultimately your decision to choose what's important to you, the following list is a good start:

1. God must be first in your life. Your relationship with Him must come before work and pleasure. You don't have to quit your job or never see the golf course again. But you must honor your commitment to the Lord to attend church, read your Bible on a regular basis, and pray every day. Attend His house first, then hop on the boat or hit the links—and take your family with you.

2. Family is next. You must take care of your spouse and children and honor them. You must teach them to be faithful to God and to put Christ first. Spend time with them, and show them every day how important they are in your life. "He must manage his own household well, with all dignity keeping his children submissive" (1 Timothy 3:4 ESV).

3. Be faithful to the church. Demonstrate a commitment to your church and attend services regularly. This will help you establish a firm foundation and strengthen your relationship with God. Attend your church's special events, such as revivals, homecomings, concerts, etc., and be active in your membership. Your dedication to your church will go a long way to help you be the Christian husband and father you need to be and will provide you with a great network of fellow believers who can help you to stay accountable in your walk with Christ.

4. Honor your country. If you live in the United States where you are free to worship, then you should thank God that you live where you do and our military forces for the freedom they have helped maintain. Freedom has a price. Our soldiers paid the price for our freedom as citizens, and above all, Christ paid by dying on Calvary to give us freedom from sin.

5. Strive to be successful in all you do. When you learn to put priorities in order, you will be motivated to become a better person. This doesn't mean you will never have stress or problems at work or school, but you will know how to deal with them better. At the end of the day, leave your work at the office, and strive to put your family first when you go home in the evening. Overtime is fine when there are important deadlines, but don't make it a routine. Time spent with your children brings you more joy and fulfillment than all the money in the world.

When you put God first, He can put all the pieces of your life's puzzle back together. And better yet, the team will be assured the right choice was made when you were picked in the first round.

DAY 22

BE BOLD AND PROCLAIM THE GOSPEL OF CHRIST

Brian Dozier
All-Star Second Baseman
Los Angeles Dodgers

By Del Duduit

We proclaim to you what we have seen and heard, so that you also may have fellowship with us. And our fellowship is with the Father and with his Son, Jesus Christ.

—1 John 1:3

"I love talking about Jesus," Brian Dozier told me in the clubhouse before the team he played for at the time, the Minnesota Twins, took on the Cleveland Indians. "It's my favorite thing to do."

He proudly describes himself as a Christian who happens to play baseball for a living. Although he loves playing baseball, serving the Lord comes first, and everyone knows that.

"My main focus is to tell everyone I meet about God's love," he said. "I've been told by some that there is a time and place to talk religion—and for me that is *all* the time. I'll talk about my Lord and Savior whenever and to whoever I meet. I have to share it because it means so much to me."

And he makes no apologies for his boldness. But he does not get in your face either. He finds opportunities during conversations to introduce someone to the goodness of the Lord.

"It always comes up when I'm talking to somebody," he added. "It's a huge part of my life. I can talk sports or music or anything, but ultimately Christ comes out."

His faith permits him to be what he is today, and he gives God the credit.

"I owe everything to Him," he said. "My faith drives everything I do."

Raised in Fulton, Mississippi, he always attended church and professed to know God. But it wasn't until the Lord began opening doors for him to play in the major leagues that his real purpose in life became apparent.

"I just started seeing things differently," he said. "I needed to have an impact on people. I needed to tell everyone about the Lord."

He developed a mentality and an appreciation for what Jesus Christ did for his life. He loves playing baseball. "It's the best job in the world," he said. "It's a dream come true for me."

But at the end of the day, if he went 0-for-4 at the plate and lost the game, if he still positively impacted one person's life, it's worth the sacrifice.

"I've been on both ends. I've had the highest of highs and lowest of lows," he said. "Sometimes you feel like a king in this game, and other times you can feel lousy."

But these lousy feelings are quickly turned into joy once you hear you made a difference in someone's life. "It makes up for all the bad times."

Being in the spotlight does not bother the second baseman. He loves the idea of being able to demonstrate and share his faith to those who are watching.

"When there are millions of eyes on you, whether it's in the stadium, on TV, or just in the community, I want them all to see Christ in me first, then a baseball player."

He also hopes they know he is a regular guy, doing a job and making a living.

Brian had a traditional childhood in Mississippi. He loved going to church and playing baseball as a youngster. On Sundays after worship services, he and his family watched NASCAR at his grandmother's home. Afterward, he fielded grounders from his dad at the city park. But the future All-Star did not use a glove. Instead, he used wooden paddles to catch the ground balls—no gloves were allowed.

"That drill made me a good fielder and taught me to use both hands," he said. "Best drill ever because it taught me the right way. It's all in fundamentals."

His desire to be a great baseball player does not match the quest to be an ambassador for Christ. He has found success in both worlds. He is an All-Star professional baseball player and a wonderful representative for the Lord. He is completely devoted to both roles.

Perhaps this explains why 1 Corinthians 10:31 became his motto. It says, "So whether you eat or drink or whatever you do, do it all for the glory of God."

"I will not do something half-hearted," he said. "I won't play baseball that way, and I especially won't live that way as a Christian. I'm all in."

On Deck

Be ready to discuss your faith openly like Brian does. You are not required to be pushy or brass, which might drive people away. Instead, show the love of the Lord inside you, and simply share what the Lord has done in your life. It's a conversation. You don't have to preach to get your point across. Slip it in at the right moment when you are talking on the job or waiting in line at an event. Be joyful, and tell others why you are happy in Christ.

Step Up to the Plate

Sharing a testimony might make some feel as though they are about to meet with the President of the United States. Relax. You are only telling others how God has made a difference in your life. Remember these three keys to giving a solid and meaningful testimony:

1. Give a brief description of your life prior to becoming a Christian. You are not required to give details or shock people, but you can still deliver your message. Tell them your life was empty and void of hope. You might have appeared happy on the outside, but no one knew the war of sin raging within.
2. Tell about the guilt and conviction God placed in your heart and how you needed to make drastic changes in your life. Tell about your exposure to the gospel message and later how it made you feel. "For I know my transgressions, and my sin is always before me" (Psalm 51:3).

3. Share how your life has been since you gave it over to the Lord. You might continue to experience problems, but now the Lord can help you deal with circumstances. Try to explain the joy and happiness you receive with knowing you are redeemed and going to heaven. Look them in the eye, smile, and tell them it's the best life ever. There are changes that must be made—but they are for the glory of God. "When anxiety was great within me, your consolation brought me joy" (Psalm 94:19).

Telling others about the love of Jesus will make you a stronger Christian. People will hold you accountable to meet expectations as well. You don't want to disappoint them, and you surely don't wish to let God down either.

You may not have the millions of eyes on you that Brian does, but if you can influence one person—you too can be an All-Star.

DAY 23
MAKE AN IMPACT ON A PERSON'S LIFE

Blaine Boyer
MLB Pitcher

By Del Duduit

> So flee youthful passions and pursue righteousness, faith, love, and peace, along with those who call on the Lord from a pure heart.
>
> —2 Timothy 2:22 ESV

Have you ever had someone in your life make a powerful impact on you? Did that person's attitude or personality change your life?

I'm sure if you reflect on this question long enough, you might be able to come up with three or four people.

Maybe you think of a parent, a Sunday school or high school teacher, or even a coach. In Blaine Boyer's case, a person he hardly knew influenced him.

He was a sophomore in high school spending time with friends at a lake house in Albany, Georgia. They were sitting around a campfire when his buddies went inside to get something to drink.

Soon, he was alone with his buddy's grandmother, who came out for a visit.

"I was looking around and thinking to myself, 'What the heck am I doing out here?'" he said. "I was a punk kid and just a disaster of an individual."

The lady began a conversation with him, but it wasn't just to pass the time. She confronted him with the gospel of Christ in such a way he had to listen.

"She talked to me out of love and from the goodness of her heart," Blaine said. "She just told me the truth about what would happen to me if I didn't get saved."

He said he had never heard the message presented to him in such a way that it "wrecked me and changed me forever."

"She told me where I was headed, and I just felt that Jesus used her to zero right into my heart," he said. "It was so real—it was like God was right there. He was locked in on my heart, and that's when things started to change for me."

Since then, his journey of faith has been a work in progress.

"I'm so thankful for that night many years ago and for her faith and obedience to share the story with me," he said. "She cared about me, even though she really didn't know me. That has always been in the back of my mind, and I try to show the same love for everyone."

Continue steadfastly in prayer, being watchful in it with thanksgiving. At the same time, pray also for us, that God may open to us a door for the word, to declare the mystery of Christ, on account of which I am in prison—that I may make it clear, which is how I ought to speak. Walk in wisdom toward outsiders, making the best use of the time. Let your speech always be gracious, seasoned with salt, so that you may know how you ought to answer each person.

—Colossians 4:2–6 ESV

On Deck

What would you do if you had an opportunity to talk to a complete stranger about the Lord? Put yourself in the grandmother's situation. You walk out to a campfire and find yourself alone with a young and impressionable teenager. Do you have enough love and boldness in your heart to begin a discussion about the ramifications of dying lost without Christ?

Step Up to the Plate

You don't have to sit around a campfire to share the good news of the Lord. You might be at work, in school, or even at a restaurant. No matter the environment, always be ready to have an impact on a person's life. Before a batter steps up to the plate, he gets ready in the on-deck circle to hit. He watches the delivery of the pitch and studies what his teammate does. He gets the timing down and monitors the situation. Now it's your turn to step up to the plate. Are you ready? Here are some tips to have an impact:

1. Show humility and compassion. You don't want to turn a person off when you speak to them about the Lord. Be understanding and not judgmental. Try to understand where they are coming from and allow them to open up to you.

2. Listen. Show them you are intently interested in what they are saying, and don't interrupt them or stop listening while you think about what you are going to say next. Allow them to tell the whole story and pray for wisdom from God on how to respond.

3. Perhaps you have a similar story to share from your life. Let them know how the Lord delivered you. Make sure they know Christians are not exempt from hard times; however, you can direct them to a God who can give them peace as he leads them through difficulties. Maybe give some examples from your testimony. But remember, it's all about God and not about you. Always give Him the glory.

4. Offer to pray with them. When you are willing to both get on your knees and, when possible, practically help carry the burden of a friend is when they know you are true and honest. Let them know you will continue to pray for them each day, and remember to follow up on your promise. Keep their names on a prayer list so you won't forget.

5. Invite them to church. Tell them about the importance of worshipping with a community of believers who will speak life into you and encourage you to press forward in your walk with Christ.

6. Stay in touch. Drop them a text, email, or a phone call once in a while. When you take time to let them know you are thinking about them, it means a lot.

Blaine had a magnificent conversation with a woman who helped to change his life. She pointed him to the Master and helped him to see his need. This is what we are supposed to do as believers in Christ. Don't back down from an opportunity to share the good news. You might be the one who makes an impactful play in a person's life and helps them search for God.

DAY 24
POINT YOURSELF IN THE RIGHT DIRECTION

Clint Hurdle
Manager
Pittsburgh Pirates

By Del Duduit

And we know that all things work together for good to them that
love God, to them who are the called according to his purpose.
—Romans 8:28 KJV

"In golf, you might be able to hit the ball four hundred yards,"
Clint Hurdle said. "But it doesn't matter if you are not lined up
correctly. The ball will go in the wrong direction."

Once Clint let God align him properly, his life started to go
down the right fairway. He knows what his purpose is now—to
be a servant and to obey the Lord.

"Life has been amazing once I realized it was going the
wrong way," he said. "I am aligned now with Christ, and my
life needs to be that of a servant."

Clint had to understand and realize this journey was not
about himself—but about the One he serves.

"Thy will be done, not mine," he stated.

He is the manager of an MLB team, and he strives to makes
everyone's job around him easier. He cares about his players
and about the people they are inside. He cares about the trainer
of the Pirates just as much as the All-Star athletes.

"I want to be a transparent leader," he said. "I want them all to know I'm here for them, and I want them all to know about the God I serve."

He shares his personal testimony often. His personal life has been well documented. The man *Sports Illustrated* once referred to as a "phenom" at age twenty remains a recovering alcoholic and has been married three times.

He married his current wife Karla in 1999. They have two children together, and he has another from a previous marriage. One of his kids is a special-needs child.

A former player and current manager, he has witnessed many of the struggles professional athletes face. He has been traded, released, and fired over the course of more than forty-three years in the MLB.

His spiritual journey has been a Christian obstacle course. "It has not been a walk in the park," he said. Yet he acknowledged God would take care of him and his family, no matter what.

Today, he finds strength in the Word of God. He sends out daily inspirational devotional messages via text and email. He confides in his "Mount Rushmore"—his personal company of men he talks with twice a month.

"I have four men, and we discuss life and our walk with the Lord on a regular basis," he said. "It's almost like a board meeting. We help each other professionally and spiritually. You cannot walk this walk alone. There must be people in your life who will hold you accountable."

He relies on these friends for guidance and support, and he finds comfort in his devotions each day.

"I have to find the time every day to read the Bible and pray," he said. "It's my source of strength."

Since Clint began living for the Lord, he can tell a big difference, and he demonstrates his testimony every day for the public to see. He is open and transparent about his faith, yet he does not force it on others.

"People know where I stand if they talk to me long enough," he said. "The Lord has been too good to me for me not to show it."

He enjoys the times he shares the good news of the gospel, and he hopes his messages will encourage and inspire those who read them.

> And whatsoever ye do, do it heartily, as to the Lord, and not unto men.
>
> —Colossians 3:23 KJV

On Deck

Are you pointed in the right direction? Is there something in your life that must be either adjusted or eliminated altogether? Clint used the golf analogy of being lined up correctly. If you try to play for a slice and hit a hook, then you will find the golf ball in the high rough or out of bounds. Do you sometimes overcompensate in your Christian endeavors? Do you let your guard down at times in fear you won't be accepted? Do you compromise your convictions to make someone feel better? Do you seek encouragement?

Step Up to the Plate

The best way to receive inspiration is to provide it to others. It will come full circle, and you will be blessed and uplifted. You have heard it said that the first thing to do when you are tossed from a horse is to get right back on him. Keep in mind the Lord has a plan for you, even when you are depressed and discouraged. Only the devil will tell you that you are not important. Defeat the forces of evil, and let God raise you up in victory. Here are some tips on how to become a beacon of light in a dark world:

1. Listen to a friend's problem. The Bible tells us in James 1:19 to be quick to hear and slow to speak. If you can show empathy and compassion to others, they will appreciate it, and you will earn their confidence. Take the time to pray with them at the end of your discussion.

2. Be honest, even if it means you must be a bit confrontational. Sometimes a person doesn't take pleasure in the truth. Take Clint's example of his Mount Rushmore, the group of men who hold him accountable. There may not be laughter and donuts and coffee each time they meet. There are occasions when you must rise and tell someone with love they are in the wrong. Provide possible solutions, and always love them and pray with them. Let them know you want the best for them, but God needs to be glorified in all things. "To do what is right and just is more acceptable to the LORD than sacrifice." (Proverbs 21:3).

3. Be joyful. Let those around you see your happiness in the Lord. This doesn't mean you won't experience problems, but it means you have faith in the Lord to see you through the challenges. If you find yourself in a sticky situation, God may not bail you out of the circumstance, but He will give you grace to sustain the consequences.

A smile can be contagious, and laughter does a heart good. "Be joyful in hope, patient in affliction, faithful in prayer" (Romans 12:12).

4. Praise. Give God the glory He deserves always. Find you own unique way to glorify the Lord, and be an encouragement to those around you. Clint does this when he sends texts and emails each day. People like to receive inspirational quotes and thoughts of hope. You can praise God on your social media accounts and spread the Word in a fun way. Find you own unique method to share the love of Christ.

There are many reasons for you to be happy and encourage others. The best one is Jesus Christ died for your sins, and you can go to heaven if you choose to follow him and accept His plan. You might have a rough path and run into obstacles like Clint did, but once you find a way to bless and encourage others, the Lord will lift your spirits. Praise the Lord in the storm and when it passes, keep on praising and thanking Him. Align yourself in the right direction, and stay the course. It's the best way to conquer life's biggest challenges.

DAY 25
GOOD IS NOT GOOD ENOUGH

Adam Wainwright
Pitcher
St. Louis Cardinals
World Series Champion

By Cyle Young

So, because you are lukewarm—neither hot nor cold—I am about to spit you out of my mouth.

—Revelation 3:16

You wouldn't necessarily pick the breakfast delicacy of chicken and waffles to be a Southern boy's favorite breakfast, but Georgia-born pitcher Adam Wainwright loves the meal. The St. Louis Cardinal has faithfully served his team since he was traded from the Atlanta Braves in 2003. And his role model is his big brother who he said "was always a source and a mentor. I looked up to him."

"He just did things right," Adam said of his brother. His influence was a positive one—he was the valedictorian of his senior class in high school and an Eagle Scout. The two attended church together with their mother while growing up, but Adam never made a decision to give his life to Jesus during that time.

"I was doing things okay," he said, "I wasn't a bad person. I was cool." But in truth, he had an unsettled spirit. And he had questions—lots of them. He wondered where Jesus fit into the broader aspects of life. None of it made sense until he attended a Pro Athletes Outreach event where he was told that Christianity is supposed to be about a relationship with the Lord.

All his life, he followed his brother's example to be a good person. He tried to do all the right things, but he was still empty inside. Although he played church for years, he was still skeptical. But Adam gained a better understanding when he realized a relationship with Jesus wasn't about what he could do but rather about what Jesus had already done for him.

He also found out that it took more than being a good person to attain salvation. His destiny did not depend on how many times he was an MLB All-Star selection or on the two times he helped his team win the World Series. Nothing he did in this world could give him the ability to be "good enough" for Jesus. Christ's sacrifice on the Cross was all that was ever needed, and when Adam finally embraced this truth, his life became another amazing testimony of God's grace.

Adam's favorite verse is Acts 20:24, "However, I consider my life worth nothing to me; my only aim is to finish the race and complete the task the Lord Jesus has given me—the task of testifying to the good news of God's grace." Sure, he's a world-class professional athlete, but first and foremost he is a child of God, and he has a relationship with his Savior. He lives his life for Jesus Christ.

On Deck

You will never be good enough to deserve Jesus. No good act or good deed you ever do will give you a special relationship with God. Christ died on the Cross to make salvation possible. Your Savior did the good deed, and He did it for *you*. Jesus died for your sins so you don't have to spend your life trying to be good enough. Humans are incapable of being good enough without the payment paid by Jesus on the Cross. His blood that was poured out solidified an opportunity for you to have a relationship with Him.

Step Up to the Plate

Does your life testify to the good news of God's grace? Would your friends and family say the way you live your life gives them the desire to have a deeper relationship with Jesus? Adam learned he could never be good enough, but he also understands he can help others find their way by finishing the race of his life strong for the Lord. If you are struggling with being good enough, use these steps to help you deepen your relationship with Jesus:

1. Place an index card on your mirror that reads: "I will never be good enough, but God loves me just the same." Read it out loud every day before you wake up and before you go to bed.
2. Pray this prayer daily: "God, help me find my value and worth in You. Allow my heart and mind to see that I don't need to be good for You to love me and instead realize I need to accept Jesus' free gift of salvation. Amen." "For the grace of God has appeared that offers salvation to all people. It teaches us to say 'no' to ungodliness and worldly passions, and to live self-controlled, upright and godly lives in this present age" (Titus 2:11–12).
3. Tell a Christian friend or mentor about your struggle. Ask questions. Share your doubts and frustrations. Ask

for prayer. It's always a good idea to have a brother or sister in Christ praying for you.

4. Read the Book of Colossians. It's an easy read, but it will help you understand that God planned to send Jesus to reclaim all humanity—that includes you—from the beginning of time. *You* are part of God's eternal plan, and He wants your life to testify about the good news of Jesus. "Therefore, as God's chosen people, holy and dearly loved, clothe yourselves with compassion, kindness, humility, gentleness and patience" (Colossians 3:12).

You can achieve a lot of amazing things in your lifetime, but like Adam, the only thing that will count eternally is whether or not you have a personal relationship with Jesus. You can expend a great deal of time and effort trying to do good things and being a good person, or you can use your life to share about Jesus and your life-changing relationship with him.

DAY 26
BE THE EXAMPLE

Tim Martin
Scout
Boston Red Sox

By Del Duduit

In the same way, let your light shine before others, that they may see your good deeds and glorify your Father in heaven.
—Matthew 5:16

"It just kept eating at me and eating at me," Tim Martin said about the conviction he was under. "Then one day, I turned my life over to Him, and it's been the best life in the world."

Tim pitched in the Pittsburgh Pirates' minor league system from 1985–87 until Tommy John surgery ended any aspirations he had to make it to the big leagues.

For ten years, he didn't even watch a baseball game on television. But in 1996, he was asked to be the baseball coach at his alma mater, Minford High School.

The Mighty Minford Falcons enjoyed success under his leadership. They won ballgames and advanced into tournament play. Life was good for him, but still he was not content.

"I'd come home after a big win and just be bent out of shape," he said. "I'd find something small and let it eat at me.

I never enjoyed the wins because I wasn't happy inside. Something was missing."

Before each game, two of his team leaders would take the team out in left field and have prayer. They set the example of what leadership was about—and it bothered Tim.

"I'd sit there, and my blood would boil," he said.

Then it dawned on him. He needed to be the one the players looked up to as an example. But instead they looked up to their teammates to encourage the team and pray for one another.

The devil was on one shoulder, and the Lord was on the other. The classic battle. Both fought for Tim's soul. "I knew what I needed to do, but I fought it because I didn't want to turn my life around."

In 2008, he gave his heart to the Lord. After his commitment to Christ, he was the one who took his team to left field to pray before each game. He still got miffed once in a while, but now it would be because a player missed a sign or didn't put forth a worthwhile effort, not because he was miserable.

All the confusion was gone, and he found true happiness. He continued to coach at Minford, and he became involved at the professional level as a scout. He later retired from his duties at the high school and became devoted fulltime to seeking out future talent for the Boston Red Sox.

Now when he reflects on the past, he is grateful for the two leaders who stood up for their convictions and set a Christian example.

> Don't let anyone look down on you because you are young, but set the example for the believers in speech, in conduct, in love, in faith and in purity.
>
> —1 Timothy 4:12

On Deck

You may be in a similar situation to the one Tim faced. He was a head coach and was expected to be the leader of the team. Maybe you are a team captain, a crew leader on the job, or an office manager. People look to you for guidance. Don't let power and authority go to your head. Instead, reflect back on the two young players who set a powerful example for their peers and inspired their coach to turn to God. Are there people who watch you and expect you to lead them? Perhaps you are a father, big brother, or mentor to young boys. Do you want them to learn about leadership from someone else or from you?

Step Up to the Plate

You long to be the spiritual leader at home, at school, or on the job. Here are some ways you can accomplish this important mission. But first, you have to want to be the leader. Once you come to this decision, consider the following recommendations:

1. Pray with, and for, your family, including parents, siblings, and children.
2. Pray with your wife. Find time each day to talk with God together.
3. Let your family see you read the Bible.
4. Read God's Word to your family, even if it's for just a few minutes. "These commandments that I give you today are to be on your hearts. Impress them on your children. Talk about them when you sit at home and

when you walk along the road, when you lie down and when you get up" (Deuteronomy 6:6–7).

5. Make decisions based on Scripture and not your instinct.
6. Rule by the law of love. Tough love is warranted once in a while.
7. Memorize Scripture and say it aloud at times.
8. Make special time for your spouse.
9. Make special time for each child.
10. Hold a family Bible study or devotion once a week. Or consider starting a Bible study with teammates or coworkers.
11. Admit when you make mistakes, and don't make them again.
12. Spend time with the Lord in private. "But when you pray, go into your room, close the door and pray to your Father, who is unseen. Then your Father, who sees what is done in secret, will reward you" (Matthew 6:6).
13. Be spontaneous and fun.
14. Do little things for your wife and be a part in maintaining the home you share together.
15. When you are forced to choose between family and career—choose family.
16. Speak life into your children and show interest in their lives.
17. Live a godly example in front of your family.
18. Get input from your wife when a decision has to be made.

19. Find men of similar character and confide in them. "As iron sharpens iron, so one person sharpens another" (Proverbs 27:17).

20. Honor and cherish your wife—your kids always pay attention to the way you treat your spouse. "He who finds a wife finds what is good and receives favor from the LORD" (Proverbs 18:22).

You need to be the one who sets the example, because your colleagues, your friends, your wife, and your family desire you to take charge. Be the one who sets the standard. If not you, then who?

DAY 27
APPRECIATE YOUR FAMILY

Matt Carpenter
Infielder
St. Louis Cardinals

By Del Duduit

Dear friends, now we are children of God, and what we will be has not yet been made known. But we know that when Christ appears, we shall be like him, for we shall see him as he is. All who have this hope in him purify themselves, just as he is pure.
—1 John 3:2–3

Being a father is more important to Matt Carpenter than anything; however, he takes his job with the St. Louis Cardinals seriously. He is on the road a lot during the season and has learned to appreciate his family when he returns from lengthy trips to various baseball parks across the country.

He never wants to make a mistake on the diamond, but he is more focused on his obligations to raise his children.

"We have a responsibility to keep a child alive, and that is pretty daunting," Matt said. "I have to provide for my family, and I want to set a good example. I have to show them right from wrong."

In order for the three-time All Star to execute this task, he must make sure he does not stumble himself. He takes advantage of his time away by staying in the Word.

"It's actually easier for me to read the Bible more because there is a lot of down time," he said, "I have more time alone, so I use that time to talk with my family, FaceTime with the kids, and become stronger as a Christian."

The 2013 National League Silver Slugger Award winner juggles the challenges of being in the public eye with his desire to serve the Lord. But he accepts his responsibilities and enjoys letting fans know he serves Christ.

"I know there are eyes on me all the time," he said. "Especially today, everyone has a camera, and I want to be careful not to be in a lousy situation. I like the fact that I'm held accountable that way."

Matt wants to be sure to put forth a positive image for baseball fans and his loved ones. He is known in the MLB world as one of the few big leaguers who does not wear a batting glove when he's at the plate. This is why his hands are often rough with cuts and calluses.

But he wants to be known as a man of God to his family and friends.

"My faith is the backbone of who I am and what I do," he said. "It's all about who I serve."

Matt was fortunate enough to be raised in a Christian home and considers himself blessed to play for a quality organization like St. Louis.

"Along my journey after college, I came to this great organization, and there are a lot of men and players who have helped me," he said. "I don't take that for granted because it could all change in an instant. I also never want to take my family for granted. I want to make sure I am the example they need to see."

But if serving the LORD seem undesirable to you, then choose for yourselves this day whom you will serve, whether the gods your ancestors served beyond the Euphrates, or the gods of the Amorites, in whose land you are living. But as for me and my household, we will serve the LORD.

—Joshua 24:15

On Deck

Do you find yourself on the road a lot with your job? Or maybe other activities take you away from the time you could spend with your spouse and children? In today's society, distractions are easy and unavoidable. But if you are committed to your family, you will find the time and a way to make them the priority they need to be. Maybe you're still in high school and you are confronted with temptations everywhere you go—on the bus, in the locker room, and even in the classroom. How can you stop following the crowd and let others know you stand for Christ?

Step Up to the Plate

If you're not yet married or leading a family, find ways to develop your leadership skills now by seeking out adult Christian mentors who can help you prepare for Christian leadership in the future. You will learn there is nothing wrong with having a successful career. Matt knows this and does his job. But when he's home, his family receives all his attention. There are business trips he must make with his professional baseball team. But he goes to great lengths to make the members of his main team at home feel like they are the All Stars. Here are some tips on how you can be the example you need to be for your loved ones:

1. Protect your house. Your spouse and children need to know you will go to any measure to ensure their safety. Pray a hedge of protection around them daily. "Have you not put a hedge around him and his household and everything he has? You have blessed the work of his hands, so that his flocks and herds are spread throughout the land" (Job 1:10). You value your possessions at home and work, and that is fine. When your family knows they are your most valued gift, you will be their All-Star.

2. Show attention and affection. There are times when work must be handled after hours, but limit the time you spend. If you are out to dinner with your wife, ignore your phone. When you attend your son's ball game, don't open your emails. They can wait. When you are in the middle of a conversation with you kids and you glance at your phone, you send them a clear message: "You don't matter as much." When you are with them, make them your priority.

3. Live a holy and clean life. A Christian husband and father must be considered the leader of his home. This does not mean you are a dictator, but you are the shepherd of your house. Demonstrate love and compassion yet enforce house rules. "Watch your life and doctrine closely. Persevere in them, because if you do, you will save both yourself and your hearers" (1 Timothy 4:16). This means live the right life in front of your family.

4. Show humility. Today's hustle and bustle world demands to be served. However, a true follower of the Lord will serve with a humble heart. When you take care of your loved ones, you show sacrifice and commitment. This

will bring admiration and loyalty from your children. Be an example to them by placing the needs of others before your own needs. Humility demonstrates leadership. "Just as the Son of Man did not come to be served, but to serve, and to give his life as a ransom for many" (Matthew 20:28).

5. Pray and praise. You might have children who are not yet believers in Christ. Or you may have some who have strayed from the faith. This can be disheartening, but don't give up. Keep the faith, present them to the Lord every day, and let them see you praise God. Don't shove it down their throats, but exhibit love and tenderness. Praise the King of kings and look for a brighter day. If your children have a relationship with the Master, confirm to them your devotion to Jesus with public praise and worship. When they see you honor your Father, they will mimic your behavior.

Raising a family is tough and takes a deep commitment. Take pleasure in time spent with them. A baseball season doesn't last long, and neither does the time your children are home. You don't want to realize this one day when they move out and you wonder where the time has gone. Take note and make them the center of attention. Go to all measures to value your loved ones.

DAY 28
GOD KNOWS WHAT HE IS DOING!

Michael Lorenzen
Pitcher
Cincinnati Reds

By Del Duduit

The LORD of hosts hath sworn, saying, Surely as I have thought,
so shall it come to pass; and as I have purposed, so shall it stand.
—Isaiah 14:24 KJV

"It just didn't make sense to me," Michael Lorenzen said. "I
was doing all the right things, but nothing was going my way."

He gave his heart to the Lord soon after he heard the gospel from a man on Huntington Beach Pier. He was seventeen
and high on marijuana at the time, but he knew he needed
to make a change. A bright baseball career awaited the high
school junior star player.

He had never been exposed to Christ before that evening on a
California beach. But he was a new creature when he went back to
school that fall. Big and strong in the physical sense, he remained
a babe spiritually, and the devil knew about his weaknesses.

Michael did not perform the way he had hoped his senior
year. He envisioned himself as an All-Star player with scouts
pouring over him to sign. This didn't happen.

"I used to struggle and think God was punishing me for some reason," he said. "Here I was trying to live right for God, and stuff wasn't going my way at all."

Other athletes who lived sinful lives yet excelled on the field baffled him.

"They would go four for four, and I'd go zero for three with three strike outs," he said. "None of it made any sense."

The 2010 MLB draft drew near, and Michael had high hopes. He pictured himself the number-one pick. Instead, Tampa Bay chose him in the seventh round. So Michael opted to go to California State University, Fullerton.

"I thought I should have been drafted in the first round," he said. "I kept thinking, 'Why is everything going great for someone else in the draft and I'm overlooked?' I knew I was better than some of those guys."

But the Lord did not overlook him. Instead, God used the opportunity to make him humble as He prepared him for greatness.

"We can turn desires of the world into things that reveal where our heart is," he said. "At that time, I was looking at those and not God. He made me see that."

In 2012, he earned All-American honors and played on the United States national collegiate baseball team. The next year, the Reds took him in the first round of the MLB draft.

He learned to wait on the Lord. He anticipated his journey to the big leagues would happen earlier, but God's timing prevailed.

"Just trust God because He is in total control," he said. "I know that now. But back then, I was confused."

He realized his own selfish behavior and attitude while in college. "God is not a genie in a bottle," he said. "He doesn't grant wishes. You have to show Him you are willing to follow."

God was in charge of the master plan for Michael's life, and He delayed his professional career because He had more work to do to mold and shape his attitude. Once that was done, the Lord delivered him in a big way. Now Michael loves to serve God, and the Cincinnati fans love him.

> There are many devices in a man's heart; nevertheless the counsel of the LORD, that shall stand.
>
> —Proverbs 19:21 KJV

On Deck

Perhaps you are in a similar situation. You make all the right decisions, and you still don't advance to where you think you deserve to be. Maybe you got passed over for a promotion or turned down for a job you were more than qualified to fill. Maybe you received a rejection from a person you felt confident was the right one for you.

In any of these cases, step back and listen to the Holy Spirit. You may feel the rug has been pulled out from under you, but that may not be the case. God knows the future, and he may be protecting you from the wrong job or a wrong choice.

The big picture is hard to see at times, but put your head down and plow through.

Step Up to the Plate

When you believe you are right, it is difficult to wait. Examine your motives, and remember the Lord is in control. While you wait on God's plan for your life, try these simple suggestions:

1. You must believe the same God who saved you hears your cries and the desires of your heart. You may pray and not receive answers. Sometimes your answer is to wait. Don't look at what happens to others. Your time will come at the exact moment God says it will happen.

2. Expect an answer. Submit your requests to the Lord, and watch and wait for His response. Don't put a stopwatch on God. He will answer in His time.

3. Dive into the Word of God. Everything that happens to you must be approved by God first, and if you stay in the Word, He will give you the strength to make it through. Use your situation to draw closer to the Lord and depend on Him.

4. Trust in the Lord. The Bible does not say you will comprehend why you face certain circumstances. In fact, it says just the opposite. You don't have to understand. Accept His way and trust. Take your hands off the wheel and let Him steer. "Trust in the LORD with all your heart and lean not on your own understanding; in all your ways submit to him, and he will make your paths straight" (Proverbs 3:5–6).

5. Be patient and don't worry. These words are easy to say yet often difficult to put into action. When you take a breath and place your faith in Him, you can set the

example and be an encouragement to others who may be facing struggles along with you.

6. Stay focused. It's only human to want to try to force an outcome. Yet in the long run, this might be a horrible mistake. Look at the big picture and wait on the Lord. Don't get ahead of Him, and don't get in the way. His plans for your life are always better than your own.

7. Stay in constant prayer. This doesn't mean to be on your knees 24/7. But it does mean to remain in a state of prayer. Set aside a special time each day to commune with God. Be consistent in your prayer life, and God will hear you. "Then you will call on me and come and pray to me, and I will listen to you" (Jeremiah 29:12).

8. Trust that better days will come. When you put your faith in man and look at others, you will be disappointed. Michael compared himself to players who were drafted ahead of him, and he became frustrated. But he waited on the Lord who prepared him for a better experience. When opportunities fall through for you, consider that God has a better ending to your story than any outcome you could ever imagine.

God is in control of your future. His way is always best. Trust in the Lord, and allow Him to show you incredible blessings are yet to come.

DAY 29
SURROUND YOURSELF WITH GOOD PEOPLE

Mike Matheny
Manager
St. Louis Cardinals

By Del Duduit

Again I say unto you, that if two of you shall agree on earth as touching anything that they shall ask, it shall be done for them of my Father which is in heaven.

—Matthew 18:19 KJV

Accountability and *responsibility* can be intimidating words. When your actions are held up to the light, consequences will result, both positive and negative.

The average fan may think it is glamorous to serve as the manager of a high-profile team like the St. Louis Cardinals. Sitting in a dugout spitting sunflower seeds and making an occasional substitution might appear to be easy to the casual observer. But this is a tireless and tedious job.

First of all, the manager has to oversee a major clubhouse and deal with the massive egos of millionaires. He has to try to appease the relentless media, and he must study and know his opponents. He is on the road away from his family consistently over the course of a long season. But his number-one responsibility is to win baseball games. In some cities, like New York, even that is not enough. You must bring home a World Series title on a regular basis.

Accountability to your employer is hard enough at times. There are deadlines to meet and duties to be performed in order to keep your job and advance your career.

Serving God can also be a challenge. Christianity may sometimes seem glamorous, but it has its own challenges, especially if you are not grounded in the Word of God.

Temptation can be ruthless and continual. It can also be disguised as glamorous and fulfilling.

God instructs us to resist temptation, and while this is the right thing to do, it is not always easy. You might have an opportunity at work to do something a little shady in order to advance up the ladder. Maybe you slip into a bar with a friend to take that secret sip of alcohol. Or perhaps you engage in lust and betrayal.

The hustle and bustle of life can be weary, and the devil tries to make the wrong choices seem right. And if you have no one to help you thwart off the forces of evil, you might not be a match for his minions. There is power in numbers. There is power in prayer. There is power in the name of Jesus.

"I personally have a board of directors that I can lean on," Mike said. "They have been there for me as far as spiritual growth and leadership."

They are also his friends. Each one holds the other accountable for their actions and looks out for one another.

This might appear to be quite a bit of work, but the results of these men encouraging each other to stay true to God and to their families are worth it.

"Iron sharpens iron," Mike said. "We have the opportunity to serve the Lord alone or surround ourselves with good people—people who are wiser and who have been around and understand the challenges we face every day."

Each man in the group is accountable to each other. They bounce ideas off each other or discuss problems they might be encountering.

When you are responsible to someone, it matters. This holds true especially if you travel and have time alone. This is when the devil knows you are the most vulnerable. You must be the strongest when no one else is watching.

"There are a lot of obstacles we face on the road, mainly during down time," Mike said of road trips. "Guys with a lot of time and a lot of money can find themselves in compromising circumstances."

Having people to account to and report to on a regular basis can strengthen your will and keep you from making terrible mistakes.

"There is always room to grow as a Christian, and we all want to do our best," he said, "I have people with me who watch me, and more importantly it's who lives within me that watches me. I need to stay sharp because there is an enemy, and I need all the help I can get."

We are all responsible for our personal actions, but it helps to have a group of friends or a personal board of directors. Helping each other through the tough times and sharing in the good ones makes sense.

> Iron sharpeneth iron; so a man sharpeneth the countenance of his friend.
>
> —Proverbs 27:17 KJV

On Deck

Have you ever found yourself in a compromising position, either personally or professionally, and looked around and saw no one was watching? There were no friends around to help you or to ask for advice. The wrong decision could have lead to a disaster or personally destroyed your reputation and even your life. Maybe you shouldn't have been in the situation in the first place. But there you were. How can you prevent similar circumstances in the future? You and only you are responsible for your actions. You are accountable. What is your next move?

Step Up to the Plate

Organizing a group of people to hold you accountable is a good idea. This is not a sign of weakness but of strength. It's a sign you do not want to mess up but want to stay on the right track and focus on the ultimate goal of reaching heaven when the game is finally over.

Establishing your own personal board of directors should not be taken lightly. Don't let it turn into a bachelor party or a golf outing. Should you include buddies? That's a tough one. I selected four men for my own personal group who I believe have the best interest for me and my family. Choosing someone you have known your entire life might not be the best selection. It has to be someone who will hold you responsible for your actions and will not hesitate to tell you the truth you need to hear.

Try these suggestions when making out the lineup for your board:

1. Pick people who inspire you. Choose those whose lives are Christian examples for others to follow, and you know they must be doing something right.
2. Choose people you can trust. You must be able to share your deepest secrets with them and trust they will keep them private. This does not have to be a confessional time together, but in case you need to unload once in a while, make sure your stories don't end up all over town.
3. Choose others of the same gender. This is not a time to be politically correct. A man should have a board made up of men and vice versa. This is necessary to avoid the appearance of evil. People talk, and you don't want to turn something inspirational into gossip.
4. Mix up the ages of your members. Strive to have a diverse age range in your group. A more mature person will obviously offer more experience while a younger person will keep things fresh with new ideas.
5. Pray about your choices. If the Lord leads you to a person, ask them. Don't worry about hurting feelings or getting the most popular person in town. This is an intimate personal growth team.

I chose my board of directors, and I'm glad I did. We hold conference calls once or twice a month. My members are scattered across a few states. I love the idea of other men praying for me from around the nation. But focus on choosing those who are right for you. A great lineup will allow you to win more games.

DAY 30
KNOW YOUR WEAKNESS

Adam Frazier
Second Baseman
Pittsburgh Pirates

By Del Duduit

No temptation has overtaken you except what is common to mankind. And God is faithful; he will not let you be tempted beyond what you can bear. But when you are tempted, he will also provide a way out so that you can endure it.
—1 Corinthians 10:13

Adam Frazier is an up-and-coming second baseman for the Pittsburgh Pirates. He made his debut in the Steel City in 2016.

He works hard to improve his craft and spends many hours in the batting cages and in the film room studying pitchers he may face. He knows dedication will pay off for him and his team.

But he is also aware of his need to become stronger as a Christian. On the ball field, he faces pitchers like Clayton Kershaw or Michael Lorenzen. Off the field, he faces another opponent—temptation.

Once the devil knows your weakness, he will exploit it and try to tear you down.

"Lust is a big struggle for me at times," Adam said. "It's not easy, but it's real. It's real for a lot of guys."

He is fortunate enough to recognize his weakness and therefore is better equipped to fend off the curveballs fired at him by Satan.

The enemy will use all forms of temptation. He uses the flesh, and he uses social media to get to his target.

"It gets to the point where you just have to quit scrolling," Adam said. "And I'm like, 'Okay, I have to unfollow this person and that person or block this one and that one.'"

He is grateful for a core group of fellow players who come to each other's aid.

"We try to be there for each other and watch out for one another," he said. "We hold each other accountable, and that is a great thing. No one wants to see a teammate make a silly mistake."

Adam appreciates the power of a consistent routine. Baseball players are known to do the same thing in the on-deck circle or prepare for a game in the same manner. The same goes for his daily devotions.

"I have my routine, and it works," he said. "I have to take time each night and do something that will make me stronger. It helps me stay on the right path."

He went on: "What comes out of a person is what defiles them. For it is from within, out of a person's heart, that evil thoughts come—sexual immorality, theft, murder, adultery, greed, malice, deceit, lewdness, envy, slander, arrogance and folly. All these evils come from inside and defile a person."

—Mark 7:20–23

Temptation is not a sin, and it comes to everyone. But it *is* wrong to give in to the devil's traps. You must know your weaknesses and cling to God for strength to resist.

On Deck

You might not be a player in the MLB, but this doesn't mean you won't face similar struggles. The devil knows the weaknesses of the flesh and will place snares in front of you to entice you to make bad choices. He may cause an argument at home and arrange for an empathetic female coworker to offer to take you to lunch to listen and talk. He may even arrange for you to receive a friend request on social media that you know you should not accept. The main target of the enemy is the family, and if he can orchestrate the collapse of your marriage, he has delivered a direct blow.

Step Up to the Plate

Adam is aware of his weakness and knows how to make adjustments to become stronger. He has a group of men who offer assistance, and he stays in his routine of daily contact with the Lord. Don't let your vulnerability defeat you. Once you acknowledge what Satan is using to try to take you down, strive to become resilient and fight back. Here are some suggestions you can use to reinforce your battle against the demons, because they do not play fair:

1. Be accountable. The Lord gives us Christian friends to support us. Mike Matheny and Clint Hurdle each have their own personal advisory boards to meet with and

discuss life issues. They hold each other accountable and lift one another up in prayer. Find a few guys you can get together with for coffee once a month, and have open discussions. They would much rather talk with you about your problems now than hear about a mistake you made later. "Therefore, confess your sins to one another and pray for one another, so that you may be healed. The urgent request of a righteous person is very powerful in its effect" (James 5:16 HCSB).

2. Hit the delete button. If you have some followers or friends who send you inappropriate messages, remove the temptation. No friend will want to break up a home.

3. Display your marriage: Make your spouse feel proud and secure by showing her off on your Facebook or Instagram pages. Make people sick of seeing the two of you and your household happy.

4. Never hide anything. If you have to hide a conversation or a text message from your spouse, then it's wrong. Stop any relationship that has the potential to destroy your family. And don't feed the rumor mill. Do not be alone with a member of the opposite sex unless she is a relative. No one should see you or your spouse alone with someone else.

5. Remind yourself of the consequences. The home is the strongest institution God established and is Satan's main target. What might have an appeal for a season will lead to a lifetime of fallout. When temptation comes your way, focus on prayer and on what is most important. "Can a man walk on hot coals without his feet being scorched?" (Proverbs 6:28).

Every player in the MLB wants to win a World Series and to improve each season. Adam has the desire to play to his highest potential. But he also wants to be an All-Star on God's team. He knows he has to stick to the basics of reading the Bible and praying every day. Will temptation come? Yes, it will. The devil has his team of liars and cheaters, and he wants to recruit you to play for him. He might even offer you a starting position and make life appear grand. But don't be fooled. Nothing is worth getting called out on strikes from a bum on the mound. Follow the Lord's will and play by His rules, and you will score the go-ahead run for your family.

ABOUT THE AUTHORS

Del Duduit is an award-winning writer and a lifelong resident of Southern Ohio. As a sports writer and former sports newspaper editor, he has won awards from the *Associated Press,* the Ohio Prep Sportswriters Association, and the Ohio News Network.

As a Christian writer, he is the author of *Buckeye Believer: 40 Days of Devotions for the Ohio State Faithful* and *40 Who-Dey-Votions for the Cincinnati Faithful* (BY Books, 2018), and he earned the Outstanding Author award at the 2017 Ohio Christian Writers Conference, as well as two more first place awards. He was also published in *Faith and Freedom* (EA Books, 2018) and is a contributor to *The Serious Writer's Guide to Writing*, pending publication by Serious Writer Inc.

His articles have been published in *Clubhouse Magazine, Sports Spectrum, Bridges*, and *PM Magazine.* He is a coeditor and writer for *Southern Ohio Christian Voice*, and his articles have been published on *One Christian Voice, ToddStarnes.com, The Sports Column, Almost An Author*, and *The Write Conversation.* His weekly blog, *My New Chapter*, appears on *delduduit.com*, and he is a contributing writer for *Athletes in Action* and *The Christian View.* He is represented by Cyle Young of Hartline Literary Agency.

Follow Del on Twitter (@delduduit) and on Facebook (www.facebook/delduduit).

Del and his wife Angie are the parents of two adult sons, Gabe and Eli. They attend Rubyville Community Church.

Michelle Medlock Adams is an award-winning journalist and best-selling author, earning top honors from the *Associated Press*, the Society of Professional Journalists, and the Hoosier

State Press Association. Author of more than seventy books with more than 1 million books sold, Michelle's book, *Love and Care For The One and Only You* (Worthy Inspired) was featured on the "Praise the Lord" program on TBN and "The Harvest Show" on the LeSea Broadcasting Network. She is the president of Platinum Literary Services and PlatLit Books.

Since graduating with a journalism degree from Indiana University, Michelle has written more than one thousand articles for newspapers, magazines, and websites; acted as a stringer for the *Associated Press*; written for a worldwide ministry; helped pen a *New York Times* bestseller; and served as a blogger for *Guideposts*. Today, she continues working as a TV host for TBN's "Joy in Our Town" and successfully running her own freelance writing business.

Michelle currently writes two devotions per month for Todd Starnes of Fox News at his website toddstarnes.com. She also blogs monthly for "Lift Up Your Day" and "Lift Up Your Day for Ladies." You can learn more at www.michellemedlockadams.com. She is represented by Cyle Young.

Ryan Farr is a collegiate coach, speaker, and pastor whose goal is to reach lost families with the truth of Jesus Christ. Having participated in both football and lacrosse as a student at Malone University, athletics have been a significant part of Ryan's walk, both in life and with the Lord—one of the root reasons for his passion for utilizing sports as ministry. For the past nine years, Ryan has been involved in coaching lacrosse (among many other sports) and local church ministry and is currently the head men's lacrosse coach at Mount Vernon Nazarene University (OH). Additionally, Ryan has been a part of creating All Out Sports, a sports ministry curriculum that promotes the skills of athletics as well as Bible lessons for young athletes. When not coaching, Ryan enjoys watching movies with his family, walks with his wife, and attending Youngstown State football games. Originally from Youngstown, Ryan now resides in Mount Vernon, Ohio, with his wife Rachel and three sons, Colton, Mason, and Easton.

Beckie Lindsey is an award-winning writer, poet, freelancer, and blogger. She is the author of the YA series Beauties from Ashes (Elk Lake Publishing) and is the editor of Southern California Voice, a division of One Christian Voice LLC, a national news syndicating agency. She is the author of devotions and a Bible study and is represented by Cyle Young, Hartline Literary Agency, and Tessa Hall is her junior agent.

Scott McCausey is the director of radio ministries at Christian Devotions Ministries. He interviews famous authors, Christian recording artists, renowned ministers and evangelists, sports celebrities, and special interest leaders each Tuesday night on Christian Devotions Speak UP! His program is also syndicated through Theology Mix ministries.

A former pastor, Scott is also the senior scientist at Eagle Design and Technology in Zeeland, Michigan. He's performed various duties throughout his twenty-seven-year career, and his vast knowledge of polyurethane allows him to answer difficult technical questions and steer new programs in the right direction.

Clint Rutledge is the son of legendary high school football coach D. W. Rutledge and went on to become an All-City player in both baseball and football at Judson High School in Converse, Texas. During his time there, he helped lead the Judson Rockets to back-to-back state championships as a quarterback on their 1992 and 1993 football teams.

Clint then went on to Baylor University where he graduated with a double major in history and English. After graduating, he went back to Judson to serve as their quarterback coach where he won his third state championship medal in 2002. In 2005, he left the coaching profession and entered the business world where he quickly became one of the top realtors for Keller Williams Realty in the greater San Antonio area.

In 2016, Clint became a bestselling author with his release of *The Classroom: Lessons on Life and Leadership from a Texas High School Football Dynasty*, which received praise from high-profile names such as Chip Gaines of HGTV's *Fixer Upper* who said, "*The Classroom* isn't just about a football program—it's about the virtues and character that truly make a person great." Former University of Texas coach Mack Brown also said, "*The Classroom* is about faith, accountability, and responsibility. It is a blueprint of 'how to' when it comes to making a difference." Finally, former NFL running back and FOX Sports analyst Spencer Tillman said, "Clint Rutledge masterfully introduces us to leadership skills that produce smarter, more resilient people."

Cyle Young is a multiple-genre award-winning author. The winner of more than sixteen writing awards, he considers himself a "binge writer" and routinely scribes thirty thousand words in a weekend. He finds great joy in writing and loves to bounce between crafting epic high fantasy tales, helpful nonfiction parenting books, and getting lost in the melodic rhythm of children's poetry.

As a former National Champion football player at the University of Michigan, Cyle takes pride that he won his first writing award for his princess picture book, *Princess Penelope*.

He serves as managing editor of www.almostanauthor.com, a website devoted to helping aspiring writers become published. He is also a monthly contributor to the parenting website, www.just18summers.com and is the co-owner of Series Writer Inc.

Cyle is a cowriter of All Out Sports devotionals and curriculums, used annually by more than ten thousand students and parents. He is a literary agent for Hartline Literary Agency. He and his wife Patty have three wonderful children on earth and two in heaven.

If you enjoyed this book, will you consider sharing the message with others?

Let us know your thoughts at info@ironstreammedia.com. You can also let the author know by visiting or sharing a photo of the cover on our social media pages or leaving a review at a retailer's site. All of it helps us get the message out!

Facebook.com/IronStreamMedia

————————

Iron Stream Books is an imprint of Iron Stream Media, which derives its name from Proverbs 27:17, "As iron sharpens iron, so one person sharpens another."

This sharpening describes the process of discipleship, one to another. With this in mind, Iron Stream Media provides a variety of solutions for churches, missionaries, and nonprofits ranging from in-depth Bible study curriculum and Christian book publishing to custom publishing and consultative services. Through our popular Life Bible Study, Student Life Bible Study brands, and New Hope imprints, ISM provides web-based full-year and short-term Bible study teaching plans as well as printed devotionals, Bibles, and discipleship curriculum.

For more information on ISM and Iron Stream Books, please visit

IronStreamMedia.com